D1293160

TAKE CHARGE
OF YOUR
FINANCES

ALSO BY JUSTIN HEATTER

The Small Investor's Guide to Large Profits in the Stock Market
Buying a Condominium

TAKE CHARGE OF YOUR FINANCES

—and win financial freedom

JUSTIN HEATTER

CHARLES SCRIBNER'S SONS
NEW YORK

Copyright © 1984 Justin Heatter

Library of Congress Cataloging in Publication Data

Heatter, Justin W.
  Take charge of your finances and win financial
freedom.

  Includes index.
  1. Finance, Personal. I. Title.
HG179.H375   1984   332.024   84–13946
ISBN 0–684–18236–X

1 3 5 7 9 11 13 15 17 19 H/C   20 18 16 14 12 10 8 6 4 2

Printed in the United States of America.

The information in this book is not intended to replace professional
tax, legal, or investment advice.

living trust

CONTENTS

ACKNOWLEDGMENTS

If I were to thank personally all of those individuals who have assisted me in bringing this book to you, I could produce a list at least as long as the Manhattan phone directory. The list would include the names of everyone with whom I have come in contact during the long years of my education and professional life. It would include those from whom I learned the fundamentals, the professionals who imparted techniques and strategies to me, the students who forced me to analyze and rationally articulate my ideas, and the loyal clients who have endured my mistakes and persistence. I can appreciate the contribution each of these individuals has made to my thoughts and career.

I must, however, single out two individuals for special attention:

David Campbell, director of Harvard's Center for Lifelong Learning, who has given me the opportunity to found and head the Program in Personal Finance which, it is hoped, will afford the public high-quality, high-principled guidance.

My wife, Sally, who once again has sacrificed evenings and weekends so that I could write this book, and who is a resourceful sounding board for my thoughts.

JUSTIN W. HEATTER
October 1984

INTRODUCTION

This book is about your money and your financial well-being. It is intended to be an eye-opener and a comfort. Don't think of it as the haughty pontifications of an oracle who has inscribed his words of wisdom on tablets. Rather, it should go down as easily as rich, luscious, premier-quality ice cream.

What do I hope I can do for you?

My goals are modest. I want to achieve the following:

- Introduce you to the arena of financial wizards and their dazzling wares.

- Demonstrate why you must take on some of the burden of financial decisions and labors yourself.

- Simplify your chores and your finances, and end your befuddlement.

- Put you in charge of your money and show you how to manage it with determination, confidence, and hope.

- Share some of my experience with you and offer you time-proven techniques for coping with financial complications.

- Tell you how to determine what's best for you instead of telling you what I think is best for you. (Of course, you will encounter some of the biases and firm opinions I've gained over the years, but I offer these lessons to save you the grief I've had to pay for.)

- Teach you the vocabulary of finance and the mechanics of using the tools available to you so that you can make the proper choices, defend yourself against salespeople, and converse comfortably with the pros.

- Help you gain the largest advantages of all in handling your money—peace of mind and financial freedom.

- Wave my arms like a cheerleader to encourage you and share my enthusiasm in the belief that you can indeed overcome.

Test me all along the way to make sure I am keeping these promises, and if at the end you don't have the rosy glow of success, call me a failure.

Why am I so cocksure that I can do the job for you?

Because I have been doing it for years for others, both clients and in the classroom.

Here's a good place to trot out my credentials.

I had the very good fortune to be educated at two solid institutions of learning at which I learned the jargon and got introduced to the workings of the financial world. The Wharton School of Finance and Commerce gave me a degree in economics, and Harvard Law School was kind enough to confer a law degree on me. Upon graduation, I accepted a position with a Boston law firm, only to find (as I had already strongly suspected) that the law had its place, but that place wasn't my territory. I struck out on my own as an independent financial adviser, was able to attract a solitary client, and built up a business entirely by way of referrals. ("Entirely" is only slightly too strong. One client picked my name out of the Yellow Pages. I told him that was no way to select a financial adviser. He told me he had been to five or six others he had selected the same way before seeing me and none of them had given him that warning. "When can we talk?" he asked. To this day, we are still talking. But the telephone directory approach is chancy at best.)

Today, as president of Justin Heatter & Associates, Inc., I am responsible for managing the money of approximately a hundred families. To do that properly, I must serve as a confidante, confessor, and financial psychiatrist as well as an astute investor. Those responsibilities helped me experiment with, develop, and formulate the methods I hope you will benefit from.

In addition to those duties, I have taught personal financial planning and investments for over a decade and am now serving as director of the Program in Personal Finance at Harvard.

Through those experiences I have learned of the great need for sincere, simplified financial guidance among those of us with moderate incomes or modest levels of assets. In an effort to satisfy those needs, I founded Quissett Corporation and the Program in Personal Finance at Harvard, and have written this book.

I must give you some warnings. I know money isn't funny, but there is so much anxiety surrounding it that unless it is approached with some humor, most people will never attack it. Anyway, I like to tease and have fun. (My wife says I should put bells around my jokes' necks so people will hear them coming.) My attempts at humor are intended not to make light of a serious subject but to make your understanding easier, to make a point more clearly, or make the lunacy of something recognizable beyond doubt. In no way is it intended to be malicious, flip or smart-alecky.

There is one other thing. I am, unfortunately, aging. Through the years I have found things that work and—surprisingly, I know—things that don't. As I've learned these lessons, and as I've aged, I've gotten to be more stubborn in my ways. Although I know this is most unusual in human terms, I must apologize for it and try to atone for it. Nevertheless, you will encounter some positions which sound harsh, unbending, extreme, narrow-minded, even possibly irrational. I have no excuse for them. I am rewarded by making money for my clients. They care not how I do it, they just expect me to do it. (Legitimately, of course.) Any approach I follow and support is one that has come out of that very basic requirement. I have no self-interest in expounding any special approach other than that I have found it to work, and have found it to work over what is a long period of time.

My presentation falls into a four-part framework. The framework, I have found, makes it easier to grasp the bewildering blizzard of financial products and services and to recognize where certain issues fit into the array.

Part One, *The Cosmos*, introduces you to the financial arena and sets your place in the universe.

In Part Two, *Status*, I take you through all of the matters that help you understand where you are today in your financial life.

Part Three, *Defense*, lets you look at those necessities which keep your financial well-being secure.

And in Part Four, *Offense*, I have you study your investment prowess and objectives, and I display some strategies I believe you'll want to consider.

PART ONE

THE COSMOS

CHAPTER ONE

HOT STUFF

Turn on your radio. Flick on your TV. Lift up your daily paper. Heft a copy of any magazine. Listen to the pounding on your eardrum as a cold caller sweetens you up or throttles you with tones of immediacy. Hoist a catalog from any educational institution. You're bombarded with messages purveying personal financial planning—either as a necessity of life ranking in importance after only food, clothing, and shelter, or as a sales pitch for a particular product or service. Taken either way, as a necessity or as a sales pitch, you're led to believe that without it you're a nobody, but with it you've got the cure for all your financial diseases and the key to financial utopia. You may even be led to believe that special potions beyond your ken are at work and that, unless you partake, you're doomed to the Siberia of destitution, never to enjoy the fruits of riches.

The truth of the matter is that in the world of financial planning, there is no new thing under the sun. True, there are, and will forever be, new products and new pitches to entice you, to make you active, to pry you loose of your loose change. No carnival barker bent on luring you into the tent can outdo financial institutions in trying to get your attention. The essential principles and most of the techniques of financial planning, however, are standard and rudimentary. Responses to new products, services, and the legal environment are required to some extent, but not to the extent that many would have you believe. Financial planning dates back to the dinosaurs.

In reality, many more of us are aware of personal financial planning and the need for it than ever before. There are many reasons for this sudden recognition. I'll give you a few of the reasons; I'm certain you can list a few more.

We are all more aware of money and its benefits and its problems than we were before partly because of all that media intrusion and partly because it's the topic of discussion at cocktail and dinner parties and at golf games as we each try to size up each other's wealth. Our incomes have gone up. It takes more to buy the big-ticket items, such as a car, a home, a college education, than it ever did before. The value of our homes has risen automatically, and it represents a significant part of our assets and a significant sum. Inflation has not only eroded the buying power of our money but it has consumed our savings and our expectations for a comfortable life in the years of retirement. Taxes have thrown us into despair. Overall, we're earning more and seeing less for it. Both husband and wife work in many families, producing income, building assets, adding complications to our money matters.

The financial institutions have detected an opportunity. They have seen these mounds of money moving about in the economy, and they want a nibble. They have devised so many new products that even they can't keep up with them. All of these new products are designed to give the developer or the seller a competitive edge. The institutions believe we're like trained rats in a maze—throw in the cheese and watch us scramble to snap up that extra little morsel. And they're cynical enough to believe that once they've got us, we won't budge except in dire circumstances. So they're all out there competing for our dollars, living by their wits, and creating new twists and tweaks to lure us into their nets. Great choices exist for us, but the choices are confusing, complex and, oh, so rapidly changing. Don't blink. You've missed a million.

The soothsayers in the legislative and executive halls of the Federal government and all the little statehouses and city halls throughout this great land have taken their whacks as economic molders. They jump here and there, willy-nilly, changing their postures as they perceive the whims of the electorate blowing thither and fro. The spine is missing from the anatomy of the political beast. Enacting laws and regulations is the cure for all monetary diseases. And reading the populace's wants is always a precise science. So passage occurs. In three years or a decade we'll find out whether or not it worked, and, well, if it didn't, no one who started it will be around to suffer the embarrassment of losing a reelection bid. Barriers to regulation fall as the strength of lobbyists increases and as the costs of elections reach ever skyward. As regulation buckles, competition heats up.

Don't get me wrong. I like competition. It benefits us consumers tremendously. I wouldn't have it any other way. I'm simply trying to explain what's causing all this hullabaloo about personal financial planning.

Communications are instantaneous. A deacon of the Anglican Church burps at afternoon tea, and the media instantly put their top minds on the situation to analyze the implications and to tell us precisely how that human upheaval affects our bank deposit and where we should run for safety or a better return. Somebody else does our thinking for us. That spokesperson casts a long shadow. Everyone falls into lockstep for fear of missing the cataclysm. And the contrived volatility and forthcoming uncertainty are murderous.

On to this relatively relaxed scene steps little ol' you. You come to this shoot-out prepared with a financial education that is appalling. (Forgive the affront. I don't mean to be nasty. I've seen too many cases of people ill-prepared by our educational system for the obligations they undertake. Regardless of age, level of education, size of income, or occupation, few of us really have been prepared for, or understand, what this business is all about.)

You enter the fray fearful, anxious, sweating wooden nickels. I don't blame you. It's like pretending you're a neurosurgeon when you've been trained to fulfill your days as a word-processor.

Relax. Calm down. Take it easy. Yawn. Most of this action is hokey. Simple things still work. Fundamentals will do most of the job for you. You don't have to be running around the streets in the altogether trying to snag that last basis point even if you don't know what it is. The world's crazy, not you. Hype is hot. Someone's going to get fleeced, and I know it won't be you.

CHAPTER TWO

THIS THING
CALLED PERSONAL
FINANCIAL PLANNING

What is this thing called personal financial planning? I'll wait a few minutes while you ponder the question.

All right. It's answer time.

I'll bet you said it has something to do with investments. Heavy investments. And I'll bet you decided that, because you're not worth a quarter of a million, it's not for you. (To this day, I remember a manager of a supermarket who had a family and was making a very good income saying, "I don't have any money, so why do I need financial planning?" He was pleased to find himself proved wrong.)

Gather round, and you will hear what financial planning is and what it can and can't do for you. You don't need a quarter of a million to play around with it. Must I say that if you are so fortunate as to have that quarter of a mill you should pay closer attention?

If you have financial resources of any kind (whether a paltry income, a humongous debt, a collection of baseball cards, a horde of gold, a lecherous heir's wishful eye, or a fifty-million-dollar portfolio of bluish chips) and you want to do something with them, anything with them, then, pal, you need financial planning. For that's all it is: Using your resources to satisfy your desires. Now you know why I said the concept dates to the dinosaurs. Lust and means have been alive since life itself. But that gets me into philosophy or archeology or some other ology, and I am ill-equipped to do battle in those fields.

Granted: the intricacies, topics, and words have multiplied, and homo sapiens has become a little more refined since the dinosaur days. But the basic needs, drives, and desires remain. We still need shelter, food, clothing. Even time away from our prowling. How do we get them? And (I thought you'd never ask) how do we pay for them? If only contemporary civilization would let us stop there. But it won't. Added to our headaches are the needs to protect what we've got, to shirk from the revenuer, to weasle in, out and around the legalistic Scotch tape of a mature society, to bury our acorns for the colder years, and to outwit the other animals to amass our bundles of goodies. Who said these are not exciting times?

These "necessities" bring us head on into such bewilderments as—forgive the expressions—estate planning, budgets, insurance, taxation, tax shelters, convertible debentures, zero-coupon bonds, closed-end funds, and other light fantastics. Well, you get the drift: Confusion. Complexity. Constipation.

Fear not, for I bring you glad tidings. All is not lost. I can bring the unfathomable to a level that even I can understand.

This entire hodgepodge, and more, because I dared not throw it all at you at once, can be fitted into a neat framework that will give your finances structure and a backdrop against which you can plot your reference points.

Point One: Gathering and organizing all your financial information is essential before anyone—you, me or another professional—can assist you with anything. This task is the killer. It is tedious, tiring, time-consuming, troublesome. But essential, nonetheless. It is the cause of the inertia many of us suffer when it comes to tackling our finances. Lick this one, and you're ahead of the crowd. Persistence pays off, I'll tell you. My cheerleader's hat is most needed here.

Point Two: Life is full of uncertainty. (Surprise!) You must expect it at any moment, and you must protect your assets (this is a high-minded book, so get that last word right) against life's uncertainties. For most of us, the mechanisms for providing protection are fairly mechanical to apply. This, quite frankly, is the most boring part of the business, both to you and to me. However, face it we must. I will take it on, if you will.

Point Three: There must be something to aim for: a goal, an objective, a reward, a payoff. Something in the future certainly, because it ain't here today. If I were to ask, "What is your financial objective?" you'd give me that same blank stare you gave me when I asked, "What is financial planning?" That won't do. You have to have direction, ambition. You have to want to achieve. Goals must be established, and we must work toward them. They are the part of this exercise that is the most peculiar to you. It is your unique combination of needs, desires, characteristics and personality that determines them. They are usually the most difficult to define with any precision.

Point Four: Steps must be taken to reach those goals. This is where the creativity comes in and the fun starts. All of us financial types have the same inventory on the shelf. How we pull it off, what we pull off, how we blend it together—that's where the secret technique comes in. Most often, these techniques focus on investing, the use of today's assets to achieve tomorrow's objectives. What makes sense? What fits? Which strategies are most likely to do the job? I'll offer some words for your consideration, most of them concentrated in Part Four.

This, then, is what personal financial planning is all about. I can boil it down to four words: Status. Defense. Goals. Offense. That's my framework.

This framework, put to good use, will make you a winner. It will tell you who you are, where you're going, how to get there, and how to watch out for the potholes in between. It's fundamental stuff. For nearly all of us, that's all it need be. And for the few others, they need it, too, even though they've moved on to all the sophisticated gyrations that accompany an overactive thyroid.

What this will do for you is put your finances in perspective and put you in control. Equally valuable, it will grant you peace of mind, let you sleep at night, reinforce your precious common sense and basic intelligence. I bring to the party a few years of experience, hopefully sound judgment based on them, independent thinking, objective guidance and some slight skill in communications.

There will not be any miracles along the way. No mystery; no mystique. There will be plain talk; simple tools; a system that works. These will help you deal with the flow of your cash, the wise use of your assets, reduction of income and estate taxes, survival for a rainy day, protection against losses, enjoyment of your retirement, the appropriateness of borrowing, and the unsurpassable pleasure of financial independence.

CHAPTER THREE

FOREVERMORE

Forget the notion that a financial plan is forever. Too often, you are made to believe that a financial plan, once developed, provides you with a blueprint that you can overlay on your life and follow in every minute detail into the dark crevices of the next century. I have seen computer-generated projections that tell you, down to the penny, the monthly benefit you will receive from Socialized Insecurity in the year 2095. Or the amount of your retirement income through the year 2017 (when either it or you expire because, whamo!, all of a sudden the projections stop). Or—and you'll like this one better—your investments, compounded at some reasonably assumed rate, will be worth $19 zillion in thirty-four years. Ah, if it were only true.

No one, with or without computer power, can project anywhere near that precisely. Yes, we can make assumptions. Yes, we can make certain projections. No, we cannot accurately foretell the future. None of us can. So don't get hoodwinked into believing that just because some black numbers appear on white paper they are indeed true. (You'd be stunned by the number of people who do believe exactly that.)

And don't get caught believing that any plan, no matter how thoughtfully conceived, can structure your affairs in a finite, fixed fashion for any long period of time. It can give you goals to work toward and can give you some ranges into which your expectations may fall. But it should not put you into a straitjacket. Think beyond it. Look beyond it. Your desires may change. Your circumstances may change. The world surrounding you certainly will change. What good will your moribound-in-concrete plan then do for you?

This is not to say that a plan has no value. It will establish some long-term direction and objectives. It will put the mosaic of your monetary jigsaw puzzle together in an organized manner. It will serve as fulfillment when you reach various closer-in achievements. It will tell you where the manholes are.

It must be as full of life, as dynamic, as the next second.

CHAPTER FOUR

TRUST ME–
I DO FINANCIAL PLANNING

Help is at your beck and call, and you may not even have to call. Everyone's into the act. Financial planning services can be provided by a lone practitioner, a mom-and-pop team, a professional with credentials in another field, a company specializing in these services, or an institution whose main jam and jelly come from selling other products or services and finds the provision of financial services an added inducement to your entering its doors. Think of the bombardment of ads I mentioned in Chapter One. Everybody's doin' it, doin' it. You can get it with your socks at the country's largest retailer. Or you can get it from the thundering herd, the country's largest securities brokerage firm. (They're bullish on America, but they may trample you.) Or you can get it from the guy on the street or on the tube.

They're all experts; just ask them.

Funny thing is, there are no requirements or barricades to anyone who wants to enter the fold. Out goes a shingle, and into business comes another "financial planner." Perhaps without intelligence, perhaps without knowledge, perhaps without experience, perhaps without standards, perhaps without judgment or perhaps with all of these traits and more. You and I have no way of knowing. We see the shingle. We need help. We trust to chance. We indulge. What do we get? We hope for the best. If we're lucky, we'll find out how well we did fairly quickly. If we're not quite so lucky, it may take several years before we learn of our wayward ways.

In any event, there is little, and in some jurisdictions no, regulation. There may not even be a definition of what a financial planner is. To put some labels on those possibilities I've suggested above, it may be an accountant, a lawyer, a broker, a banker, an insurance person, or a candlestick-maker dressed in other garb. And how are you to know about his, her, or its qualifications, ability, or performance? You may be sprayed with alphabetical collections of many varieties: CPA, CFA, CLU, JD, CBS. Each of these (save the last, which snuck in) indicates a level of expertise and accomplishment in some field. But not necessarily in financial planning. The argument is made: Each of these professionals (whether human or institutional) may have his, her or its own economic ax to grind or may not be au courant with the latest techniques or information. Maybe yes, maybe no.

To counteract these failings, there has come on the field of battle a fairly new breed of cat. He/she/it is supposed to be a generalist, a knower of all disciplines, a person who can cross party lines to make proper recommendations for you regardless of possible allegiances. This person, too, is called a financial planner. Some have gone so far as to obtain their own designation: CFP. The letters stand for "Certified Financial Planner." Certified by whom? By a correspondence school. And many of those who have obtained this designation are reborn insurance or securities sales-people who have cloaked themselves with the costume of apparent objectivity only to sell the same old products from a new vantage point. Of course, no group is all bad. There are, indeed, some good souls in this bunch as there are some good souls in any tribe. And to further legitimatize the industry, many real schools and colleges are now offering certificates and degrees in financial planning to those successful candidates who complete the curriculum. The curriculums obviously vary with the institutions and the instructors, as they do in any other field of education.

Where does this leave you? Bewildered for sure. Not knowing what to choose or even how to choose. Throw darts? Pick up the Yellow Pages? Buy by looks? Rely on referrals? That seems the best way, but it may not be the best way. You come to me as a potential client. You ask me for some references. I give you the names of two or three clients. Whose names will I give you? Those whom I've maimed or those whom I've made millionaires? You contact the millionaires, and they tell you what an absolutely terrific guy I am. You come in the door, and we go to work. Let's hope I make you, too, into a millionaire. Granted, with references your odds have improved. I'm saying only that an improvement in odds is all that you can expect, not an absolute guarantee of unwavering integrity and uncountable success. Put another way: Without it, you've got nothing; with it, at least there is some likelihood you're on the right path.

CHAPTER FIVE

THE BOY SCOUT MOTTO

I am great. I am good. I'm as clean as Checkers. (If you're too young to get the reference translate that into "a hound's tooth.")

Those are the cries you hear from every financial planner. Without question, implicit in these comments is the implication that the other planners ain't. Forget the claims. Ask yourself: What characteristics would I like to find in my financial planner? And then, after making out your list, answer this one: What is the probability that I will find them?

For your consideration, here is my list of characteristics.

I'd like my financial planner to be:

- Accessible—Reachable when I need him.

- Decisive—Makes decisions easily and gives me clear-cut choices

- Experienced—He's done it before.

- Friendly—I can warm up to him and maybe even get a chuckle.

- Honest—Imbedded with integrity.

- Independent-thinking—Not beholden to one interest group or another and not swayed by extraneous influences.

- Inexpensive—Fairly priced, giving me value for my money.

- Informed—Alert and abreast of the times.

- Knowledgeable—He knows the facts, products, ropes and rules.

- Loyal—Appreciative of a long-term relationship.

- My man—He works for my interests and not his own.

- Non-intimidating—I'm not overwhelmed by his stature, structure or attitude.

- Objective—He can make decisions based on my needs rather than his pocketbook.

- Professional—He conducts himself with dignity and propriety.

- Rational—He exercises sound judgment with little or no emotion.

- Respectful—Treats me as a human being and doesn't lose sight of the fact that it is my money.

- Responsive—Doesn't take four weeks to get me my information and responds to my requests in a timely manner.

- Sensitive—Evidences warmth, understanding and humanity.

- Stable—He's there today, he was there yesterday, and he'll be there tomorrow.

- Thorough—Watches the details and the big picture and is comprehensive in his survey.

- Thoughtful—Goes out of his way to look out for my interests.

- Trustworthy—Capable of accepting confidences and cash with equal degrees of respectfulness and responsibility.

- Understandable—He talks to me in the same language I speak.

I think that's about all I'd want in the way of characteristics. In addition to those characteristics, I must add, I'd want him to make me some money. I can't overlook that aspect.

You may have other concerns. Feel free to add to my list.

Once you have, I must leave you with a question. It's the same one I asked in the second paragraph of this chapter: How likely is it that you will find all of these attributes in one place?

CHAPTER SIX

A QUESTION OF COST

Compensation for the provision of financial planning services is received in one of two ways: on a fee basis or on a commission basis. Under the first method, there is an agreed-upon fee. This fee may be set at the rate of such-and-such per hour, or it may be a flat fee for the total job. Under the second method, you may never see your charges. The person with whom you are working gets paid a commission for selling a specific product (such as a tax shelter deal or an insurance policy), and you may never know what compensation he was paid. In many instances, those who get paid on a commission basis may give you "financial planning" services free of charge. For example, an insurance agent will take all of your numbers, run them through a computer at his company's home office and come back to you with a multi-page printout wrapped in a sterling binder all for nothing. Can you guess that somewhere in that binder there will very likely be a recommendation for you to buy more insurance?

Which is better: a fee-for-services planner or a commissioner? In theory—and this is what the fee-for-service individuals will tell you—when you are paying a fee they can be entirely objective and can suggest products and approaches which are proper for you, instead of selling you products you may not need simply so they can get a higher commission. You are buying their time, expertise, judgment, independence and lack of potential conflict of interest. In theory, fine. But in reality, who knows? Why do I say this? Because one never knows how these people act or what kind of ties with others they may have. I'm a professional in the field and many times I cannot tell. Through working relations or through deals, it is possible that your planner may be receiving referral fees, finder's fees, split commissions, favors, or trips to Barbados. Legally, the planner must disclose these benefits. But it is usually done in an off-hand way with the result that you can't claim non-disclosure, but the presentation and timing is such that it is slanted to obtain the desired defusion. Again, my point is not that it always happens this way, just that there is the possibility of it happening and that you may have some difficulty in discerning it.

Fee-only service can run $50 to $200 an hour and fees may total anywhere from $1,000 to $10,000 for the entire performance depending on the complexity of your situation. Is there any way to reduce these fees? Would I ask if there weren't? The more effort you put into the data-gathering routine, the more you will save. (We all know your time is "cheaper" than everyone else's.) You can spend time organizing the materials, summarizing the facts, or completing checklists of information or questions so that when you go to the pro you will reduce the number of hours he must spend on those chores. Some pros present you with a detailed questionnaire for you to complete. This will accomplish the same purpose. You may, if the questionnaire is thoughtfully prepared and written in your language, even learn a great deal from this fundamental task. And then the next big labor-saver is for the pro to take this questionnaire data and pump it through a computer. Not that the computer can make intelligent judgments. But it is most effective at churning out numbers. And this, believe me, not only saves a professional's time but also ensures a standardized quality of review and the prevention of a lapse in memory. Computers used in this manner are efficient time-savers and impersonal screens. They should be used to satisfy those objectives and have their printouts submitted to the professional for the exercise of his judgment.

Now we shall consider the commission-paid planners, those reputedly sinister fellows who sell you their highest-commission products and who run that conflict of interest risk. Their response to these accusations is that you are going to have to go somewhere to have your plans implemented, that you are going to have to pay somebody these sales dollars, that they sell the full line of products you may ever need, and that they will stand with you on your side throughout eternity to cement a binding relationship. Valid points. The uneasiness you must address is whether in fact what you are sold is what is "best" for you or is simply the high commission ticket item. As anywhere else, it depends entirely on the salesperson and his value system.

If you use one of these commission-paid types, you may also encounter forms and questionnaires and computer printouts. They are used to save the salesperson's time just as they are used to save time for the fee-only planner.

For insulation against the evil claims made against them for potential conflicts of interest, some commission-paid planners are using the services of an independent company which provides the review of your data. They will point to this as an objective appraisal of your affairs and then sell you the products suggested in the appraisal. This way they offer you objectivity, unbiased analysis and the ability for them to implement the recommendations. Usually, this appraisal is based at least partly on a computerized analysis which results from your completion of a questionnaire.

So much for the costs of planning. Let's look at the costs of non-planning. What could it cost you if you don't bother with this undertaking?

For a list of horror stories without putting actual dollar amounts on them, try this: Not being able to overcome a budget deficit. Borrowing too much or on too costly terms. Not having enough available assets. Not having the safety in your investments that comes from proper diversification. Having investments which don't meet your objectives or which aren't performing for you. Paying too much in taxes. Not taking advantage of some basic, non-risky tax-saving devices. Having an outdated will or estate plan. Paying too much for the wrong kinds of insurance. Being underinsured in some vulnerable spots. Facing retirement with inadequate dollars.

That list will give you some thoughts on what planning can save you. I leave it to you to estimate the amount of your own hard-earned money you could be burning up by not doing some planning.

CHAPTER SEVEN

THE ULTIMATE
FINANCIAL PLANNER

Would you like to meet the ultimate financial planner?
Good.
Take out a mirror. Go ahead, look into it. Who do you see?
Why, of course, it's you.
Surprised? I know it is surprising. But here's my reasoning.

My firm belief is that no one walking the earth is closer to, knows more about, cares more about, is better equipped nor is more deeply involved in your financial affairs than you are yourself. No one can be, nor would you want him to be. You are the one who can pay the most attention to what you're doing and can even be on top of it every second, if you choose to be. Those are advantages that you cannot pass on to others. Others can do an adequate, but not superbly outstanding job because they are not up to the minute every minute. If you want that kind of superior attention, you must look inward.

"Hold on," I can hear you plead. I can hear your protests coming. I know you're not professionally trained to make financial decisions. I know you don't have the time. I know you're not confident. I know you're not familiar with each single word and concept. I know you suffer from inertia. I know you have other demands on your time from your family and your primary occupation. I know every other excuse you could throw at me. But hear me out: All I'm saying so far is that you are the most appropriate person to pay the greatest attention to your own money. To the extent that you don't pay attention, you'll regret it. Stay in there, stay alert, no matter whom you choose to help you.

Your choices for assistance are three: (1) You can hire a professional on a fee or commission basis. (2) You can do everything yourself. (3) You can hire a professional to do some of the work, and you can do some of the work.

I have already made noises about turning to a professional for the whole thing. Outstanding ones are hard to find. They are expensive. There may be added problems. The probabilities for success run against you. You must be involved to some degree. (Even if you choose to go this route, read on. You'll get ammunition to defend yourself against some sales pitches and some professionals.)

The problems with doing it entirely by yourself may, I recognize, also be great. Earlier I dismissed your excuses out of hand. I did it to make a point. I know they represent real issues and concerns. But, to the extent you are interested, determined, confident, I believe you can do approximately 90 percent of this financial planning stuff yourself. Basically, it is common sense. No professional has a monopoly on that. I would, however, reserve the territories of estate planning and intricate tax planning to the accountants and attorneys. I hope I'm not biased in their favor because of my own background. But those areas, I believe, require some pretty heavy duty technical know-how. If you lack that competency, you try them at your peril.

With your common sense and good intelligence (you bought this book, didn't you?), I'm sure I can get you to that 90 percent milepost.

I'd like to say a few more words as to why I believe it is essential to involve you in the process. Notice the name of the area we are discussing—personal financial planning. There are three, not merely two, ingredients to consider. You may emphasize the "financial" and the "planning" aspects and skip over the "personal" aspects. I do not. For me, they are by far the most crucial.

I have said earlier that all of us financial types have the same products on the shelf waiting to be chosen. The appropriateness of the choice centers on you: your needs, makeup, likes, fears, hatreds, anxieties, expectations, responsiveness to risk levels, and a ton of other issues too personal to mention in print. I can guide you. I can pull those products off the shelf. But, unless you are comfortable with the mix, you're not going to be successful in your plans. Call it financial psychiatry. It is at the core of all financial decision-making. Who knows you better than you?

Smile. You've just taken on the title of "the ultimate financial planner." Not that you can do it for others. Just that you can do it for you.

CHAPTER EIGHT

TEMPUS FUGIT

Time is the bane of our existence. It is the one item we all share in common. It is also the thing that we always have the least of. The passage of time is the only thing that makes me tense, that causes me to worry. If time is so precious, why squander so much of it on financial planning?

There is an assumption in that last statement. The assumption is that this effort demands considerable chunks of time. Well, I won't deceive you. Initially, to get yourself together, you'd better prepare for a siege of somewhere between ten and twenty hours. (You do not have to do it all at one sitting. You'd become part of the chair if you sat straight through that length of time.)

And be reassured. Most of that time will be spent searching out the relevant records from your shoe-box collection or other archival repository of family valuables. Once you locate the shoe boxes and their vital documents, you will have to shuffle through papers you would rather ignore, like wills and insurance policies. Face up to the task. You will have to take it on only once, and then it will be history. You may sneeze a little from the dust, but there should be no lasting harm.

The task of searching and shuffling is usually the most time-consuming. There is no way of avoiding it, short of turning it over to a servant at the going wage. Don't tackle it all in one night. Try to fit it in between a few personal hygiene commercials while your intellect is being stimulated by television. Make it a contest of endurance. Reward yourself with a licorice upon emptying out each of the shoe boxes.

Having completed this monstrous chore, you will feel virtuous.

Your conscience has been telling you that you should have taken on this job before. You just didn't want to face it, like that broken light-switch you've been meaning to fix every Saturday for the last fourteen years. Enjoy feeling virtuous. Gloat in your accomplishment.

With all those materials collected, you will be ready to organize your information. I'll show you how to do that in the next part of this book. Plugging the information into the correct slots soaks up less time than gathering it. Once more, take it in stride. Spread it over a couple of evenings so you don't get bored.

Zap! I've just wiped ten to twenty hours out of your life. You're young enough not to miss it. Anyway, it's for a good cause.

After you're organized, very likely you'll have to make some adjustments. Give me about five to ten hours for this. Most of this time will go to playing telephone tag with salespeople or professionals and listening to spiels. A necessary part of your education. Again, once done, done. Subject only to fine tuning and readjustments from time to time as needed.

We're in the home stretch. Barring a hyperactive investment agenda, minuscule amounts of time spent policing and tinkering with your affairs will be required. Keep the responsibility in the rear compartment of your brain, but schedule a couple of hours at the end of each calendar quarter for a review. This is so you don't get into your old rut of ignoring your financies. Shirk that quarterly update and your monetary state will again be adrift in the hateful condition I first found you in. The only thing worse than a sinner is a backslider.

PART TWO

STATUS

CHAPTER NINE

WHO YOU ARE

Status is something we all seek. It salves our egos. It makes us feel important. It balloons our self-esteem. It distracts us from our failures. We like being recognized by the headwaiter. We like being the smartest student in the class, the wealthiest guy on the block, first on the moon, "number one." I'll pass no judgments on those ambitions, I'll accept them as givens.

I'm dealing with status at a more mundane level. Many of those ambitions are desires we must aim at and work toward. Many of them, but certainly not all, result from having a nest egg of piled-up bucks. I'm starting from the here and now—the level you are at today—and then we will try to pile up the bucks to get you to the level of real meaningful status where you can be queen or king of the hill.

What must we know to determine where you are starting from on this ladder of self-aggrandizement? Think for a moment about the sort of information you would need to paint your current financial portrait. I'll give you some time to collect your thoughts and write down the types of items we must know to explain what you look like financially at the starting gate.

OK, I'm ready. I hope you are.

There are items on my list that you would probably not regard as financial. These include considerations such as your age, health, marital situation, dependents, potential responsibilities for others, expected inheritances or the possible receipt of significant gifts. By focusing on these factors we are able to place you in the wash of humanity and locate you in the universe of financial parameters. Also, there are other factors, more typically financial, in this list of what you may perceive to be only personal factors. Your occupation, your current earnings, your potential earning power, the years you have left to sweat it out in your sweatshop. And on and on. All of these considerations tell us who you are and what factors may have impact on your financial planning. I can do no more than make you aware of their significance. They are all vital to the development of a financial plan.

Turning to those matters which are purely monetary, my list becomes much more substantive. We must know the sources and amounts of all your income, where you spend your money and how much you spend, the property you have managed to accumulate over the years, how and when you acquired it and who owns it, the obligations you've built up and the terms under which you are expected to repay them, how you appear to the tax collector, what perks accompany or did accompany your paycheck, what kinds and amounts of insurance are standing in the wings waiting to be called on in a time of need, and the legalese embodied in the four corners of your will and trust (if any). Those items will fix your portrait financially. Some I will deal with in this part, others I will defer to the next part.

Let's now see how handsome or (and I must be very careful with the choice of this next word) pale you appear.

CHAPTER TEN

INTO EACH LIFE
SOME ASSETS MUST FALL

We begin our analysis of your financial portrait with a study of things you own—your assets. Assets are different pieces of property, tangible or intangible, that you have acquired over time and which you now own. The pieces of property have a present value, and you can control the use and disposition of them. You may have acquired the specific piece of property by buying it, by inheriting it, by receiving it as a gift, or by theft. This last method I can't offer any advice on. The first three methods are important to keep in mind for they may have different income tax consequences when you go to dispose of the asset.

Before I send you off to make a list of your assets, let me give you some clues as to what you're looking for. Take this tiny test:

Which of the following are assets?

A print purchased at Woolworth's.

A Rembrandt.

A share of stock in General Motors.

A condominium.

A mortgage you took out to acquire the condominium.

The bill for your vacation.

Last month's pay.

My copyright on this book.

Your bank account.

Your life insurance policy.

Your MasterCard balance.

The money you laid out for this week's groceries.

Money in your retirement account.

The bric-a-brac decorating your residence and the clothes on your rack.

The scooter you use to play in the traffic.

In literal terms, the list of assets would include the Woolworth print, the Rembrandt, the General Motors stock, the condominium, my copyright, your bank account, the life insurance policy, the money in your retirement fund, the bric-a-brac, clothing and scooter. I have deleted from the list the condominium mortgage, the vacation bill, and the MasterCard balance because these are obligations which must be paid. We will encounter them in the next chapter. I also excluded as non-assets last month's pay and the money invested in this week's groceries because I will presume that those funds were consumed. If they weren't, then they, too, would represent assets.

I take a jaundiced view of what an asset is for financial planning purposes. I narrow the category down somewhat because I'm thinking of assets not so much in a strict sense but rather in a "usability" sense. Which assets have current value and can be turned into cash or another asset that will permit me to start building additional value or to produce more income or to save on my taxes? I chop away those assets from the list we just developed that don't appear to meet this criterion. Good-bye to my Woolworth print, the bric-a-brac, the clothing and, alas, the scooter. If any of these had some special value according to the terms I just described, I would retain it on my asset list. For example, maybe among my bric-a-brac is a Chippendale chair or an antique desk, or maybe my scooter is a classic Mercedes that has appreciated in value. In those instances the property in question has a value separate and apart from the personal use value. It has a distinct market value which I may be able to realize if I were to sell the item. In that case, I would count it as an asset. If I were to sell my Woolworth print, my sofa, or the clothes off my rack, what would I get for them? De minimus. True, they have value for me. But they have no significant market value nor even a significant market.

There's another message here. I am making some judgments. I am saying that some things are assets, and then I am saying that some of these assets are not to be considered as assets for our purposes. I have excluded those that are owned more for personal use than "investment," those that have very low market values, those that have no "market" in which to be sold. I would also exclude those that you do not have current access to, or over which you have little or no control or cannot get at without some major complication. The money in your retirement fund would be on my list in this category. This money presumably has strings attached to it, is there only for a limited purpose, may not be reachable by you or may be reachable but have some heavy tax deterrents connected with its release. Other items in this category could be certain types of trust funds or employee benefit plans other than retirement plans.

You can see the judgment calls I'm making. You must make an adjustment in your thinking. A great number of all decisions made in finance (let alone financial planning) are judgment calls. The scope of these calls can be narrowed down. But the final decision is made on your judgment. Nothing scientific or formula-determined.

Part of what I'm looking for when I ask for a list of assets is the facts, only the facts. Another part of what I'm looking for is to see where changes are possible. And then I like to explore what the consequences of making those changes would be on an asset basis, an income basis, and a tax basis. (My wife says I run our lives like a portfolio, always looking for changes. I confess I'm guilty.)

From the group of remaining assets I will prepare a presentation that breaks the assets into two major headings: liquid and non-liquid. Liquidity is the ability to convert an asset into cash. The more liquid the asset, the easier it is to convert to cash; the less liquid, the harder. Nothing is more liquid than cash because it already is cash.

What is the significance of liquidity? It tells you not only the ease with which an asset can be converted to cash, but also may tell you the likelihood with which you would choose to turn it rather than some other asset into cash and the price you might receive in doing so. It is necessary to consider the ease with which you can convert an asset into cash simply because you may need the cash. You don't want to get caught with your cash down. There are bills to pay. There are merchandise and possessions to buy. There are homes to acquire. There may even be investments to make. And, to paint the dour side for a moment, when death occurs, there are bills to be met and taxes and costs to be incurred. For all these reasons, liquidity is something to keep your eye on.

Another side of the liquidity issue is the probability that you will, in fact, turn an asset into cash. There are two points to consider here. The first is: Because of your personal needs or wants, how likely is it that you will sell a specific asset? You are more likely, for instance, to sell a stock than your residence, more likely to sell a piece of investment real estate than an interest in a private business, and so forth. The second is somewhat related to this consideration and has some influence over it: How broad is the market for the asset you are selling? If there is considerable activity in that market and if there are many investors in it, I would suggest you are more likely to consider selling the asset than not, only because you will know that you are more likely to receive a "fair" price for your asset.

Allocating assets to liquid and non-liquid categories and ranking them within those divisions on the basis of their relative liquidity entails further judgments. For some of us the cash sitting in a life insurance policy will be a liquid asset and for others of us it will not be. For some of us the shares of stock in a named company will be liquid and for others of us they will not be. For some of us our home has less permanency than it might for others. For some of us the Rembrandt will hang on our wall until death do us part, and for others of us it may become boring. Further, our perceptions of the market and therefore the potential sales price we may receive for the Rembrandt may differ.

On my list of assets there remain the following: the Rembrandt, the share of stock in General Motors, the condominium, the copyright, the bank account and the life insurance policy. Within the constraints of judgment I recently mentioned, I will divide those assets into liquid and non-liquid and attempt to rank them within those divisions by their relative degrees of liquidity. Here they are:

Liquid

The bank account
The share of stock in General Motors
The life insurance policy

Non-liquid

The condominium
The Rembrandt
The copyright

Please note: I included the life insurance policy among the liquid assets. It may or may not appear there, and it may or may not appear on the list at all. The nature of a life insurance policy is that it pays off what is called its face value (the dollar amount of the contract) when someone (called the insured) kicks off (and I don't mean in football terms). Some policies offer only "pure" insurance: the premium you pay is lost if the event doesn't occur. Think of your car insurance. You pay the annual premium, and after the year is over, you pay another premium for another year's renewal. "Pure" life insurance works the same way. Another type of life insurance has not only the insurance feature built into its premiums, it also has a cash accumulation feature built in. Under this type, every year you pay your premium, you are paying a portion of it to cover the insurance feature and another portion of it to accumulate "savings." This so-called accumulation of savings is known as the cash value of the policy. It is this number, if it exists under your policy, which should be included in the list. It is the dollar amount of accumulated savings which is there sitting and available to you if you want to borrow it or cash in the policy before you pop off. (You can get this figure from your policy or by calling your insurance agent. Expect a lecture if you make the call.) The face amount of the policy is, in reality, a contingent claim in that the dollar amount can be recovered only by dying and therefore should have no value as an asset until it is actually collected (at which time, of course, you won't be here to list it or to enjoy it).

There are a few other factors we must consider when we are making a list of your assets.

The first of these is a notation of who the actual owner is. Ownership has a great deal to do with what can be done with an asset, who owns it on the owner's death, and the implications of income and estate taxes. I will discuss those matters in due course. For now, let's leave it that property can be owned in an individual's name, in a couple or several names, or under a name that the law recognizes as a separate entity (for example, a trust). At this point, while making out a list of assets, it is important to show who owns what.

Next, for those assets which can appreciate or depreciate in value, it is wise to show the date you acquired them and their tax "cost" on the list. On assets that don't change their values, such as savings accounts or certificates of deposit or regular bank accounts, it is not necessary to list aquisition date and cost. Such assets grow only by having interest added to them; they do not change their underlying spots. Where, however, an asset is of a type which can have a change in its value, its acquisition date and cost are important considerations when it comes to taxes. For now, if you will take my word, it is necessary to note on your list the date you acquired the asset.

The "cost" figure depends on how you acquired the property. If you bought it, the cost is the price you paid for it. That figure may be increased by certain costs you incurred when you acquired it—for instance, brokerage commissions on the purchase of the share of Gereral Motors, or the legal fee on the purchase of the condominium. It may also include costs you incurred after you acquired the asset. For example, if you put some major improvements into the condominium, the cost of those improvements would be added to your cost. Your cost may be reduced to a number below that which you paid for it. Take, for example, the condominium. Assume you rented it to someone else instead of occupying it yourself. Each year you owned it, you would reduce your taxes by an amount allowed for depreciation (a maneuver I will demonstrate in Chapter 41). To the extent you have depreciated the condominium, your "cost" will be reduced. So, you can see, when you purchase an asset, its tax cost can be what you paid for it, what you paid for it plus certain costs incurred on its acquisition and, if it's real estate, plus any improvements or less any depreciation.

If you acquired the asset through inheritance, the question of your tax cost is easy. Your tax cost is the amount at which the property was included in the estate of the person who left it to you. What could be simpler?

If you obtained the asset by gift, your tax cost is the same as the tax cost of the person who gave it to you. That is, if you are going to show a profit when you sell the asset. If there is no profit, the government wants you to bear the brunt of the loss. The number you can use for your cost is, generally speaking, the number which will produce the smallest loss (either the giver's tax cost or the value of the asset at the time of the gift).

Why is all this tax cost business important? Because it establishes the benchmark from which any profit or loss is calculated for tax purposes in the event you sell the asset. Depending on the asset's cost and the time you held it, certain tax implications flow. I'll give you a full, but simplified, explanation in a later chapter.

On your list of assets, you should obviously show the approximate current market value of each asset. This can be a close approximation. The only reasons for precision are to insure certain types of assets (such as jewelry, when an appraisal is necessary) and to come up with a value for estate tax purposes. Other than in those two circumstances, your best guess as to current market values is good enough.

Once you have the current values, I like to know what each category represents in relation to the whole. Take it from me, the total of your assets equals 100 percent of your assets. What percentage of those total assets does each item represent? To find out, divide the total dollar value of your assets into the value of each specific asset and multiply the answer by 100. This percentage figure will help you understand how well you are diversified when you are considering some investment allocations and possible moves. (If, by chance, you have six bank accounts or twenty-nine stocks or fifteen government bonds, you may wish to list them on a separate schedule and include only the totals on the list we are currently discussing. Whatever works for you and makes the presentation clear is what counts.)

Finally, you might want to note somewhere on your list the indicated amount of income the asset is expected to produce on an annual basis. For instance, if you have $1,000 in a bank account that pays 5 percent interest annually, you might want to put a notation in parentheses right after the back account's name ($50) so you won't forget that it is expected to produce that amount of income over the next twelve months.

I would like to put all this gibberish together for you in an understandable form. Here's a table containing the assets we've been discussing.

ASSETS

Item	Owner	Date Acquired	Cost	Current Value	% of Total Current Value
Liquid					
Bank account ($50)	Me	—	$1,000	$1,000	1
GM share ($4)	Spouse	1974	75	70	0
Life ins. (cash value)	Me	—	1,000	1,000	1
Non-liquid					
Condominium	Joint	1980	30,000	50,000	50
Rembrandt	Joint	1979	5,000	45,000	45
Copyright	Me	1984	—	3,000	3
Totals			$37,075	$100,070	100

I listed 0 percent for the share of GM since it represents such an insignificant amount. And, clearly, the Rembrandt is postage-stamp size or it would have a greater value.

My apologies for making this chapter so long-winded. We have laid a lot of groundwork. You now know what an asset is, what "tax cost" means and why it's important, something about life insurance, something about ownership alternatives, a little about estate taxes, and how to make a table reflecting your assets and allowing you to manage them. You've also gotten a confession that most of the decisions made in financial planning are judgment calls. That's what I'd call a good start on taking charge of your finances.

I've yapped enough. It's time for action on your part. Whip out a piece of paper and make out your own list of assets. You'll find the experience enlightening. Most likely, you will discover you own more than you thought.

CHAPTER ELEVEN

PAYING THE PIPER

Getting into debt takes no talent. Anyone can do it. You find something the brothers Brooks are selling, and you just gotta have it so you charge it. Thirty or forty days later you wonder where the money will come from. You ring up a night out on the town on your 'Merican Express card to the tune of $250 'cause you didn't leave home without it. And the next morning (even before the thirty or forty days pass), you awaken with a head throbbing in rhythm with the beat of the dollar rather than last night's band. Or you take out a personal loan to buy a refrigerator. Or you visit one of those many-digit finance companies. Or you borrow a bushel basket full of moola to buy your home. Or, easier still, you run up your telephone bill to the level of the satellite spinning 'round the globe. As I said, it takes no talent to mount up the obligations. We are in a credit society. Credit is there for the taking, the almost too easy taking. And one reason it is so easy is that (no kidding) some people, the lenders, make a nice amount of change from lending. Quite likely, if they are selling merchandise or services, they're making more on the interest you pay than on the goods and services they sell. It goes without saying that if their business is selling money, they make money or they won't be in that business long.

Getting out of debt does take real talent. Many of us can't handle it. Either we don't have the ability to withstand further temptation, or we don't have the self-discipline to pull ourselves out of the hole. Or the sums get too astronomical for us to wrap our minds around. Or living with globs of debt becomes psychologically comfortable. Or, worse yet, we believe it's "smart" to borrow or that it's a great tax dodge.

I'd like to slay a few dragons. Debt is not all goodness. If may even be dangerous for your financial health. When should you use it? What are its benefits? What will it cost you?

I'll hit the last question first. Using credit will always cost you more than paying cash. (There is one exception to this blanket indictment: If you charge to your charge account of credit card an amount you pay at the time you receive the bill, credit costs you nothing. Its cost, without doubt, is built into the price of what you acquired, but that's a philosophical discussion.) Borrowing from sources other than parents always entails a slight charge for the use of the money. The charge is known as interest. If you're going to play this game fairly, it is expected that you will repay the obligation plus the interest on the money owed for the time the money was owed. The total, you will find, as in algebra, is greater than the amount you borrowed.

How much greater? It depends on the interest rate charged by the lender, the time for which the loan is outstanding, and the method in which the interest rate is computed. Take a modest example. Assume you borrow $1,000 for one year and agree to repay that amount plus "simple" interest of 8 percent per annum (per year, for you non-Latin scholars) payable at the end of the year. (This method of calculating interest is the most favorable to you.) Quick. What's the interest? Yep, $80. In naked numbers, it doesn't sound enormous. If you were to talk in terms of $10,000 instead of $1,000, the interest could start to look like real money, however. Under our example, you borrow $1,000 and pay back $1,080, the $80 being the cost of the use of the money for a year. You're out of pocket an extra $80. Or, turning it around, whatever you used the money for cost you $80 more to buy. (I have clients who still think it sinful to pay cash for a car in spite of this lesson. If you want a lesson for your own information, take the total payments on any loan you have, subtract the amount borrowed and stare at the difference. C'mon back after you faint.)

Not to worry, you say, because the entire $80 is deductible on your Federal income tax return. Yes, sir, the entire amount is deductible. But the deduction saves you on your taxes only the proportion that is equal to your tax bracket. (I will define what a tax bracket is in a later chapter and will show you how to determine yours. For our purposes here, let's just say that your tax bracket is the rate at which your next dollar of income will be taxed by the Feds.)

To show you what I mean, follow this explanation: You pay out in cash that $80 worth of interest. On your tax return you deduct from your income the same $80. But, because, let's assume, you're in the 30 percent tax bracket, you will "save" only 30 percent of the $80 or $24. "Saving" in this sense means that you will not be paying that sum in taxes. In truth, you will be laying out all of those $80. Instead of paying that $24 to the Feds to help them run their own deficit efficiently, you will be paying it to your lender for being such a nice lender. The whole $80 goes out. Instead of giving $24 of it to the tax people, you give all $80 of it to your lender, and this shortchanges the tax people by the same $24. Put another way, you must put out $80 of interest and this "saves" you from paying $24 in taxes. The day ends with your being net out of pocket $56.

Is paying interest on a loan a good way to save taxes? Not in my book, and that's what you're reading. Others, of course, say otherwise. But, as you can see, the shibboleth that paying interest eliminates income taxes is a tale too old even for wives. I grant you, there is the chance that because of your huge interest payments, your tax bracket might fall. But here, too, the savings are not dollar for dollar, simply a few more pennies higher per dollar.

So why borrow? Because you can't in any other way afford to buy something that you just have to have. (You need a new scooter, and you've plain run dry of cash. You need a château, and the tag is higher than your cash reserve. You spot a bargain on a snowblower, and the tab will be higher in December than it is in July and you don't get your bonus until the eve of Christmas.) Because, if you don't buy it now, inflation will drive its price out of reach when you're ready with the greenstuff or, alternatively, what you buy with the borrowed funds is expected to appreciate and to do so at a rate which is higher than your cost of borrowing. Or because you can make money on the "spread" between what interest you have to pay and what you can get for your money by investing it somewhere. (Now we're starting to sound like bankers, for this is what they do, pay less to get it than they lend it out for.) I'll give you one "for instance." Suppose you have one of those cash value insurance policies I mentioned in the last chapter. If your policy is several years old, you will find you can borrow your cash value at the rate of 5 or 6 percent. If it's a newer policy, you will find the rate will be 7 or 8 percent. You can find the interest rate by looking at the loan provisions in the policy. Even at the top of these rate ranges, you may find that you can borrow the money from your insurance company and reinvest it at higher rates. At the lower levels, I will guarantee that that will be true. There are several other reasons why these funds are sitting ducks for you to shoot at. One is that there is no requirement for repayment. You can let the balance sit there and never repay it. If you follow that course of non-action, the loan will be "repaid" at the time of your death by taking the amount owed out of the face value of the policy.

Think not so much of the aspect, but of what that money could be growing to if you invest it wisely. A corollary of the no-repayment thesis is that you can relax mentally. There is no cloud around your brain pressuring you with the thought of having to make those periodic payments or that big nut of a payment. You can watch the days slip from the calendar without worrying how much your daily interest charge is or where you'll find the money to make the payment with when it comes due. For you may not even have to make the interest payments if your cash value keeps building in adequate numbers of dollars and if you don't want to deduct the interest from your taxes. What could be sweeter?

Implicit in some of these comments has been the fact that I would not borrow for purposes of consumption. Skip the debt for vacations, clothes, iceboxes or lunch. Borrow only for investments. That is, to acquire assets that you expect will appreciate in value or produce a higher return than you're paying. For the kinds of assets we were talking about favorably in the last chapter. Plus one other that you may not regard as such—yourself. I have in mind doing such things with borrowed money as enhancing your own future by taking advantage of business opportunities and education. These are investments in a different sense, but they are investments which should produce handsome rewards.

When I borrow, I like to borrow as much as I think I will need for as long a period of time as I can get at a fixed interest rate. By doing that, I am in control of the loan. I have the money tied down. I know what my repayment terms and schedule will be. I can plan for them and adjust my affairs accordingly. I should not have a gun at my head.

I will have to pay an interest rate that is competitive today when I borrow the money. If interest rates go up, I can sit here and chuckle at the poor saps who have to go out begging for loans at the higher rates, smug in my knowledge that I was a superior planner. If rates go down, I will be sad. Sad unless I can reborrow the money from the same source or elsewhere at a lower rate, pay off the then outrageously expensive loan and be free of my sadness. This rewriting of a loan depends on several considerations. One is any charge I might incur for prepaying the original loan. (Some lenders make a penalty charge for early repayment because they were counting on having the money earning interest for the expected period and because it costs them money to put the loan on the books.) I might incur extra costs in making the transition. (For example, charges for credit checks or legal fees.) I might be concerned with the new terms, the new relationship, or the new restrictions placed on me. Let me say I prefer the kind of loan I described for the reasons I've enumerated. The decision about rewriting a loan can be made only by calculating the numbers—the total number of dollars that will have to be repaid over the future of the comparative loans, the timing of the payments and the amount of each, the costs of getting from here to there, and the net saving or additional cost.

Loans with "floating" interest rates are not high on my hit parade unless you can turn them to your advantage. These loans adjust the interest rates charged on a periodic basis based on the changes in some benchmark defined in the obligation. When you start talking of a ceiling on the potential rate, the lender typically starts talking about a floor. The provision of both in the loan document is not unusual. The reason for using the floater is that lenders have learned just as you and I have that inflation is a possibility. They don't want to be locked into a 3 percent interest rate when current rates are at 19 percent. A reasonable position, you'd agree. Rather, the lender would like to transfer the risk of rising interest rate levels to you since you're undoubtedly better able to withstand its monstrous weight. To entice you into taking on this risk, the lender may give you an extra inducement to select the floater over the fixed rate. (Everything's marketing.) He may say, for instance, you can have the money at a fixed rate of 8 percent, but if you take the floater, you can have it at (an initial) 6 percent. On the surface, it's a good deal if you don't worry about how high is the sky. It's a function of time and money. If you expect to pay off the loan before its interest level catches up with and exceeds the fixed rate loan (you'll have an estate settlement or a bonus, or you expect to sell your condominium in three years when the rate, by the loan terms, can't go up more than half a percentage point a year) you know which to choose.

Floating or variable-rate interest is only one of the spangles in the exciting new world of lending in the '80s. All kinds of bells and whistles are being added to the traditional standard loan approaches to make it easier for you to borrow, and maybe even repay. Be wary, careful, thoughtful.

From the "which are assets?" list at the beginning of the previous chapter, I would like to bring to your attention three examples of obligations requiring repayment. These are examples of things you owe which, in technical jargon, are known as liabilities. The three items are the mortgage on the condominium, the bill for your vacation, and your MasterCard balance. We must collect some information about each of these so we'll know what to expect and how to handle them in our financial dealings.

Clearly, we'd want to know what the current unpaid balance on each is. How much do you now owe? What interest rate is charged, when is it charged, what is it figured on, and how is it calculated? What payments are required at what points in time? What additional terms should you be concerned with, such as any prepayment penalty? Is there any collateral pledged to secure the loan? If so, what is it and what constraints are there on it? (The more volatile in price the underlying collateral, the bigger the stick of dynamite you are sitting on. Watch that when borrowing with stocks as collateral.) I would gather these details (and I ask you now to gather them on any obligations you may have) and then I would list them in a table as shown on page 48.

Having frozen these obligations on this table, what do we do with them? We have to consider repaying them. As I did in discussing assets in the last chapter, I am going to take a narrow view of where and how we show these obligations. I like to keep my list of current bills in one place and the longer-term bills or the ones with significant balances owed in another. The vacation bill and the MasterCard balance seem to be small enough amounts (and the indication is that they are currently due or soon to be due) that I would show them in the expenses I am planning to pay within the month. (I will discuss these types of expenses in a later chapter.) They are distinguished from the long-term expenses in that they are due currently and they are

LIABILITIES

Obligation	Interest Rate	Periodic Payment	Other Terms	Balance
Mortgage	8%	$292.19 (Mthly)	Last paymt due 11/91	$20,279
Bills	—	—	Total due next month	$560
MasterCard	—	—	Total due now	$311

manageable out of currently available funds. The longer-term obligations, or those having significant balances, I like to list in a separate table. They represent the heavy load I must face up to. What is longer term? Anything that will stretch over at least nine more months. What is significant in terms of balances due? Something that you cannot possibly pay out of currently available funds, something that, to you, feels hefty. I know these comments leave you groping in vagaries. They're the best I can do. I fall back on my earlier comments about personal considerations and judgment calls. The main value in making out your list of significant obligations is the recognition it confronts you with. Where you put it is not immaterial but neither is it necessarily terminal (although the debt itself may be).

How much debt or liability can you afford to carry? The answer is not fixed. Generally, it comes down to what amount of payment you can afford to carry on a current basis, that is, how much expense money you can lay out on a monthly basis to meet your obligations.

For curiosity's sake, and only for that reason, you can tote up your obligations and take the totals as a percentage of your total assets. Using the above figures, and taking the license to round them to an even grand, the number I come up with is 21 percent, figured this way: $21,000 obligations divided by $100,000 assets (from the previous chapter), multiplied by 100 to make the result a percentage.

There you have it. What do you do with it? Realize that your debts equate to 21 percent of your assets. If your assets are chewed away by your obligations, 79 percent of your assets will remain untouched. If the proportions were the other way around, you'd realize that you have problems. The breaking point depends upon how much you feel the pressure (and on how much income you receive to support the weight hanging over you).

CHAPTER TWELVE

THE NET EFFECT

In Chapter 10 I had you collect a list of your assets and other incidental information. In Chapter 11 I had you gather together those nasty bills reflecting your liabilities. I am going to put far less of a work load on you here. The assignment for the few paragraphs which comprise this chapter is so undemanding that even a child can do it.

Subtract the total of your liabilities from your total assets and you come up with a number that is known as your net worth. Put in other words, this number represents your net assets. "Big deal," I hear you snort.

Don't be so difficult.

For us financial weirdos, the concept of net worth is important. It is one of the three most meaningful facts that help us place you in the cosmos. If you have a negative net worth (liabilities exceed assets), that unfortunate state tells us one thing. If your net worth is $26,000 (to pick a number), that tells us something else. If your net worth is $526,967 (to pick another number), that tells us you're the kind of person we'd like to deal with because there is enough there to make our attention to your affairs worthwhile.

Before taking up the negative net worth and modest net worth situations, let me add to the large pile of objections I gave you earlier in the book about how improbable it would be for you to get aid. Speaking of net worth: them that has got can get. The well-to-do can not only afford to hire the over-$100,000-a-year salary types, but those types are more likely to pay attention to people having a large net worth. Partly, it's a matter of time and money. If you have something in the lower ranges of net worth, chances are high that I will have to devote as much time to straightening you out as I would have to dedicate to the better-off soul. Maybe, in fact, even more time. Who, I ask you, will generate more fees for me? And be more equipped to pay them? On a measurement of my time commitment then, I'm better off with the high roller. Another admission: The more loot you've got, the more I can do for you. I know that's not news, but I want to put it on the table to reinforce your non-professional conclusion. If you have more, I have more opportunity to spread the money around, to experiment with different things, to maneuver with more leeway—and to survive more mistakes.

If you're in a negative net worth posture, the first thing I would have to do is to reduce your debts or to increase your assets. Pronto. Because your net worth tells me that you're on the ropes financially, and unless we pay immediate notice to the primary problem you may be in terminal straits. Even though we've only recently become acquainted, I don't want that to happen.

If you're in a modest net worth posture, the cure is the same— reduce the debts or build the assets—but the time pressure and the immediacy of the problem are not as overpowering. We very probably have more time in which to build your net worth, so we could employ different tactics. Perhaps we could squeeze more out of your income to put into investments or to pay down debt. Perhaps we could invest differently to get better tax breaks or improve the investment rewards. Perhaps we could reshuffle the debts to reduce their costs or uncover hidden nuggets of beneficial changes.

Earlier, I said that your net worth is one of the three factors that give you a quick position-fix in the financial universe. The other two are your total annual income (How many bucks flow into your paws each year?) and your tax bracket. (Remember the chapter on assets that you thought you'd never get through? I'm going to continue to let you dangle on this one until I get to a later chapter and confront the tax issues head-on.) If you or I can determine these three facts about your finances, we can place you fairly accurately in the financial cosmos. The determination of your net worth, to repeat, is one of those factors and that is one of the reasons for calculating it.

There are others. One is merely to tell you whether you are on the negative or positive side of the line. As I've said, this indicates what kind and degree of surgery that may be required. Another reason is to measure the scope of the money available for manipu-lation. Another is to give you a glow of comfort (or indigestion). Yet another is to hint to us financial types both the amount of net assets we have to work with and what those net assets are. For instance, you have a loan outstanding against your car or your home or your securities or the cash value of your life insurance policy. I can tell how much slack (borrowing space) is left vis-à-vis the asset under scrutiny, or which assets are left free and unencumbered; that will aid me in making decisions.

What amount of net worth is adequate? Ah, but if it were only that straightforward. Here's all I can say: First, it should be positive. Second, it should be large enough to keep you happy. (You get the drift of where I'm heading already, don't you?) Third, the more the merrier. Fourth, even if you're merry, I may not be. I want to build it up as rapidly, as consistently, but as prudently as I can in every way I can. That is the object of the whole show. Building capital. Capital provides security (to con-firm another cliché). It buys financial independence. And that's the biggest reward of this exercise.

Now that I have you hyped, I must throw in a clinker. Your net worth also gives us a gauge (inaccurate, but approximate) of what estate-tax concerns you (really your estate, since you'll no longer be with us) will face at the final curtain. More will follow on this subject you can rest assured, and even in peace.

The suspense has built long enough. Go ahead and do your subtraction and see what your net worth is. And be prepared to be pleasantly pleased.

CHAPTER THIRTEEN

SNAP!

You've just taken a snapshot of what you own, what you owe, and what you're worth at a given point in time (now). Those are the elements of a balance sheet (like the way I snuck that technical term in on you?) and that's what a balance sheet does. It shows those three items as of a given date.

So why all the excitement? What can you do with it? How can you use it? Will it manufacture cookies or produce rapture? Hardly.

It has three basic functions:

First, it will educate and inform you. By preparing it, you will see what you own, where you stand, the rest of the details. This results in your peaceful mental state. It will also enable you to look at the current results and ask yourself, "Is this where I should be? Where I want to be? Is this a proper allocation of my resources?" It will communicate to you an indication as well of where change is demanded, desirable, or possible, and what the consequences of those changes might be.

Second, it will present you with a means of comparison. You have completed your first balance sheet as of this date. Next week, next month, next year at December 31, you may decide to do the chore again. By laying one balance sheet beside another you can see what changes have occurred between the two dates. Are you making progress?

Third, it will give you an objective to work toward. Let's say that today you decide you have too much of your assets in bubblegum wrappers and you conclude they are too sticky to be liquid. So you decide that at a date twelve months distant you would like to have no more than 2 percent of your assets in such trivia, or you decide that you'd like your obligations to decline to only 93 percent of your assets from 99 percent. You could project what a balance sheet would look like at that time and draw it up. Then you could step back to the reality of today's balance sheet to study where there is flexibility that will allow you to work toward those objectives. How many dollars can you move? Which assets can you move?

Personally, although these functions do not produce cookies or rapture, I believe they should turn you on.

CHAPTER FOURTEEN

DOLE WITH THE DRUDGERY

The subject of this chapter is the benefits that accompany your paycheck—so-called employee, work-related, or fringe benefits. Don't overlook them for the bearing they have on your financial situation. (If you're self-employed, most of this is not for you, but you might hear me out and get some ideas on how the rest of us survive.)

I refer to such benefits as "footnotes" to your balance sheet. They lie in waiting, to be called upon in a moment of need. They tend to have no current value, but do have a contingent value: in the event of such-and-such, you are entitled to such-and-such. Some benefits may have a current value, but you may not have access to it without jumping through some hoops or turning the produce wagon over. Either of those activities may limit the height of your desire.

A few words brought to you by your employer: None of these benefits are appreciated—not in the groveling sense, but in the comprehension sense. The existence, meaning and importance of them doesn't get through. They are taken for granted, are expected, assumed. Their absence angers, but their presence is for naught. Yet the provision of these benefits costs your employer an additional 37–40 percent or so of your paycheck. If you get paid $1,000 a year (and sometimes it feels like that's all you're getting), the cost of these benefits to your employer can run another $370–400. Benefit costs have been rising rapidly. The red tape with which some of them are tied has become more snarled and costly. The result? Where some benefits have not been previously provided, they are not being added. Where benefits have previously been provided, some are being dismantled. Where a limited menu of benefits has previously been provided, some employers now offer a cafeteria plan of "flexible" benefits: you can choose the benefits you want from those offered. Where benefits have previously been provided, employers are trying to find alternatives to offer you which might achieve similar end results but which reduce costs and administrative snafus and potential liability. In short, matters have run out of control, and contrived solutions are being brought forth in response.

From your side of the bargaining table, these benefits have tremendous worth. Not only do they represent an additional 37–40 percent in "pay." They come nearly always in non-taxable or deferred-tax terms. You pay no current income tax on them; you may never pay an income tax on them. This is the way to go. If you had to purchase them with after-tax dollars, you would need much more than that 37–40 percent extra to cover the cost because you would first have to incur the tax. Stay with that 30 percent Federal income tax bracket I gave you somewhat earlier. To end up even-money on replacing the cost of benefits that were costing your employer 40 percent of your pay, you would have to receive an extra 57 percent in pay. It's cheaper to do it the normal way. Even where you must contribute something toward reducing the cost of these benefits to your employer (or where you can voluntarily buy more through your employer), it's far less expensive to obtain the benefits from this source than it is to go out on to the open market as a sole shopper. Employers have clout. They are sold better packages than you and I could obtain ourselves. They are easier for salespeople to sell, service and handle than a bunch of us yo-yos. The costs of selling and administration are reduced to the provider, and those reductions (or most of them) are passed on to us by our employers.

On all of these benefits you should know: What specific benefits are available to you? What are their specific provisions? How and when do you qualify to participate in them? What do they cost you, and, if more than nothing, how much? Are they "portable?" (Can you take them with you if you leave—for any reason —voluntarily or otherwise?) Can you convert them to your own contract when you leave, and if so, how and on what terms and at what cost?

Nearly every employer has shiny little brochures which explain these topics to you. Fear not to lift them up and open their covers. These days, nearly none are written in polished legalese. Supposedly, they are written in twelfth-grade English (which is more than many lawyers have been able to master). You can collect your brochures from your personnel department and prop open your eyelids to protect them from drowziness. Pretend the brochures tell you about Tahiti or some other exotic land, and you'll get to the end of them still thinking about running your toes through that soft, warm sand. You may even encounter some drawings or cartoons in the brochures. One trend is to write them in comic book form so there will be no question that you and I can relate to them and understand them. Captain Marvel was never so much fun.

If you don't get the point of all these brochures, or if you're stranded with further questions, attack your personnel person or department. They're used to it and expect it. Their jobs wouldn't be there if they didn't have to do it. They innately recognize they will have to deal with us on the Mickey Mouse level so you will be fulfilling their expectations if you go in at a dunce's level. You will be doing them a favor by doing so. You will in no way be showing your ignorance or intimidating yourself or ruining your macho image. The vernacular in this arena is something else. Acronyms become verbs, doublespeak filters through a lens of metaphor. Get it? I don't either, but they do. Ask them. It's their job to explain it all to you.

CHAPTER FIFTEEN

A SMORGASBORD OF GOODIES

Take your plate and join me in line at the country's largest not-for-free lunch. The sampling of goodies will tempt your palate without necessarily tempting your purse. The selection seems endless.

We start the delectables with your working environment. Sure, if you're lucky, you're encased within four walls (one or two possibly with windows), a floor and a ceiling. You'd be absolutely certain an employer would provide those. Many employers have gone beyond the minimums to locate their cubicles amongst greenbelts, on lakesides, in picturesque settings, and have piled lush carpeting on the floors, added soft lighting, and supplied Vivaldi concerti grossi piped through their Muzaks. Those luxuries make the setting more conducive to labor and are thought to add extra profitability and productivity to your efforts. But, as facetious as I may sound, environmental factors cannot be ignored when it comes to considering your workplace. You spend most of your day there, and if the setting smells, so will your attitude. Taken one step further, think about your exercise room, sauna, health club, real cafeteria (with subsidized menus permitting you to gobble a four-course lunch for 89 cents and saving you from having to make supper when you get home), lunch hour fashion shows or musical entertainment, yoga classes, Smokenders, stress-reduction workshops, seminars on turtle breeding and natural childbirth. All of this to make your work experience more attractive. The food, I would hope, is nutritious and the others helpful to your physical or mental well-being. Maybe some might improve your skills.

Then there are the coffee breaks, the extended lunch hours, the nineteen paid holidays a year, the eight "personal" days you can use to go to the racetrack or the psychiatrist, the vacations and some of the "downtime" spent replaying last night's basketball game. Hey, the time off may be only slightly less than equal to the time on. And all this without a worry as to the continuity of the business or its profits.

Now we get to the real meat of the matter, the insurance coverages and the money-accumulation modes. Every employer offers some sort of medical insurance program. Usually, these programs provide both basic coverage for the payment of medical expenses incurred by you and what is called master or major medical coverage, which extends the basic protection to many additional types of charges. In some cases these programs have an unlimited ceiling so that you will never run out of coverage, no matter how high your medical expenses go. Add in coverages for maternity, psychiatric, detoxification, dental and whatever treatment comes with the next fad, and you can see how extensive is the security blanket. Recall, too, that these benefits cover you, your spouse, and your dependents under most plans (and even if you incur a slight fee for the extra protection extended to your spouse and/or dependents, the levy is very modest).

There usually are benefits that will continue to pay your salary for some period in case you are unable to work due to an illness or accident. I'll ignore those statutory programs such as worker's compensation which are required by a socially-conscious electorate. Here I am speaking of a salary-continuation program. It may take one or both of two shapes. There is the short-time solution which pays you for X-number of sick days annually or goes somewhat further and pays you for, say, up to six months if you become disabled and can't work. Then there is the long-term solution which steps in at some point (after six months, as a possibility), and provides benefits running for an established number of years. The idea behind these programs is to replace your lost pay. Other than the very short-term types, none will give you your full salary (or allow for any increases in what you receive after you are out). Most normally, they will pay you no more than 50 or 60 percent of your prior pay. The theory is you have to be bludgeoned into working, and if they made it too appealing to you, you'd never go back. Shows you how little they understand our true motivations and dedication.

Life insurance is quite frequently thrown in. At the bare bottom rung, an employer will give you a policy equal to your annual base pay. Gratis. (Some will pay for two times or four times your base pay.) Over what's free, you may be able to elect to purchase additional coverage (up to a limit) at a greatly reduced cost. It can be a good deal.

Other good deals on the insurance front are the possibilities of homeowner's or automobile insurance made available through your employer (but paid for by you). This is merely a "source" for such insurance for you to consider. The money saving comes from having the insurer pass his savings on selling and administrative costs on to you through the employer.

Coverage under governmental programs such as "socialized insecurity" may be mandatory, but they should not be ignored. Neither should they be totally relied upon. Social Security has many faces. Under its Medicare provisions it provides medical expense coverage to those 65 and over. It provides benefits for you if you are totally disabled and unable to work. It provides death benefits for your dependent survivors. And it provides something for your retirement years. This broad range of potential benefits must be factored into your financial thinking (and very likely has been factored into your employer's).

Up to this point, nearly all of this has been a tax-free ride. Yes, you must make your contributions (how's that for a euphemism?) to Social Security. But on the receiving end, none of these benefits should be taxable other than your salary, money you get for your disability insurance that you didn't pay for and, possibly, some life insurance. Not bad at all.

The area of pension planning is one that is fast changing. The traditional approach was to have the employer create and pay for a fully fleshed-out plan that, on paper anyway, would take care of your needs in retirement. The traditional approach started to come to an end on Labor Day of 1974 when then-President Gerald Ford signed something known as the Employee's Retirement Income Security Act. He did a good deed. ERISA, as it is known, made some revolutionary changes on some substantive issues that had led to horrendous results for far too long. For example, it made sure you had a pension after putting in your required time; that your pension would indeed be there regardless of whether your employer was or wasn't; that you could leave your job and take your pension benefits with you once you were entitled to them; and that there would be no shady dealings or shenanigans with the funds in the pension. It did not, however, require that an employer have a pension plan. It merely said what he'd have to do if he did. Further, ERISA had some procedural requirements that tended to be expensive and nuisance-creating. The violation of them could lead to some severe liability problems for the employer or the plan's administrator.

Employers found the red tape expensive, nauseating and threatening. They found the pension plans costly. Those that had no pension plan decided to stay outside the fold. Many of those who had a plan decided this game was no longer for them, and so they terminated their plans. Those who remain stick by the book to a "T."

In lieu of pension plans employers adopted new tricks or emphasized old tricks that had new meanings. Profit-sharing plans took on new lustre. These are plans which may in the end provide retirement benefits but which do not require a contribution from the employer until he has exceeded a threshold level of profits that he has defined; he then contributes a set amount of those profits. If you're in the plan, you have an interest related to your years of service with the employer and your pay. The advantages for the employer are apparent. No profit, no contribution. Costs that can be contained. Less red tape. More incentive for the workers to produce a profit. Loyal and dedicated workers. For you, the advantages relate to tax savings. The money thrown into the plan is not taxed to you until you receive it later. The money thrown into the plan earns additional money, again on a tax-deferred basis. The dough compounds quicker because it isn't suffering the intrusion of taxes.

Some employers provide thrift plans. These encourage you to set aside a set percentage of your salary (generally 2–6 percent, your choice—there are limits) in another type of tax-favored account. Your employer contributes his share along with yours, usually half of what you put up. The money you put in is taxed before you put it in, but it accumulates in a tax-deferred fashion similar to the results under a profit-sharing arrangement. The money your employer kicks in is not taxed to you until you take it out. Both sets of funds gather additional dollars on a tax-deferred basis until taken out.

One of the newest wrinkles is something called a 401k plan. The reference is to a section in the Infernal Revenue Code bearing the same number. If your employer adopts such a plan, you can set aside generally between 2 and 12 percent (your choice—there are limits) of your base salary. Your employer may match some part of this contribution. The money that both you and your employer put in is not taxed until you receive it at a later date. Once again, the money in the plan gathers moss on a tax-deferred basis.

Should you toil for a not-for-profit organization (meaning it was established that way, not that that's the way it turned out in practice) you may, if your employer has adopted such a plan, sign on for a joy called a 403b plan. Again, the reference is to the Code (not Hammurabi's). There is a limit on how much you can put into it based on a formula which takes cognizance of all your pension benefits. The consequences of your participation are the same as for the 401k plan. The rubric for this type of plan may be either a Supplemental Retirement Annuity or a Tax-Deferred Annuity (SRA or TDA to the cognoscenti).

The thinking behind each of these plans is to encourage you to save your money and to do so on a tax-favored basis. The reason is quite understandable: To have you yourself make up for, replace, or supplement the declining pension rewards emanating from employers or the Feds. No sweat. The responsibility for your retirement needs has always been on your shoulders, you just never recognized it before. The incentives are there, usually in the form of tax savings or deferrals, sometimes in the form of employer assistance.

(I want to insert a fleeting reference to a variety of stock option or stock ownership plans made available by some employers before continuing on the retirement track. These plans can be extremely rewarding to you and may have some tax breaks along with their rewards. The variations are too numerous for me to deal with in a cursory form. The reason behind them is obvious: Incentive. Go to it.)

A further recognition that you must take steps to plan for your own retirement was contained in the 1981 Economic Recovery Tax Act. (Love those monickers. I don't know where they get them, but they're always a mouthful and ring of the noblest tones. And there's at least one a year.) ERTA, the Act's acronym, opened the door to every worker throughout this great land to establishing his or her own Individual Retirement Account (IRA, for the uninitiated). This account can be established by you if you have any income generated by your sweat (that is, other than investment income). You can set aside in such an account every dollar you make up to the first $2,000 ($2,250 if your spouse doesn't work. At least $250 of it has to go into one or the other's account). This can be done regardless of whether or not you have any other retirement plan or plans. It is available to every worker who provides services for pay, and this includes those of us who are self-employed. (Welcome back, fellows.)

Self-employeds, attention! You have your own deal. You can establish something known as an HR-10 or Keogh plan to provide for your retirement. (The "HR" stands for House of Representatives, which is where the bill originated, and the "10" was its number. "Keogh" comes from the name of the lovable Brooklyn congressman who proposed the bill. Any other trivia you'd like to learn about? Send your questions along.) The amount you can put into such a plan is limited to the smaller of 20 percent of your net self-employment income or $30,000 a year. Other than that limitation, the IRAs and the Keoghs work the same way.

(To stimulate your thinking and to make some work for tax attorneys and accountants, in using the dollar limits for the IRAs and the Keoghs I have been using the approach of something called the "defined contribution" method. This calculates the permissible number of dollars you can put in based on your current earnings. The alternative method, known as the "defined benefit" method, measures the dollars you put in in terms of the benefits you want to take out. This is figured on actuarial assumptions and, at some ages or at some income levels, may entitle you to set aside more dollars currently than under the defined contribution method.)

Money put into an IRA or Keogh plan is not taxed until you take it out. Money that money earns while in either of these plans continues to earn money on a tax-deferred basis until you take it out. When you take it out, you may be able to gain some further tax breaks by juggling the way you take it out.

Money placed in an IRA or a Keogh plan can be withdrawn starting anywhere between age 59½ and 70½, at your election. It can be taken out earlier if you become totally disabled or die. (In the first case, you'll be glad you have it. In the second, you'll not be here to enjoy it.) The money can be taken out at any other time subject to a penalty. All the money will be fully taxable at that time, and there will be a penalty tax of 10 percent of the money you take out. Don't let that stop you automatically. Weigh the benefits of the tax deferral against the cost of taking it out, and make an intelligent decision. Just because there is a cost to be incurred, does that stop you from going to the movies?

The decision about making contributions to any of these plans —thrift, 401k, 403b, IRA, Keogh—depends on a number of personal factors and factors specific to the plan. The major determinant is: Can you spare a dime? I mean, if your budget (and we'll get to that next) has no slack in it, you're whistling Dixie cups to consider contributing. If there's no slack in your budget, you can't afford tax savings. Or putting today's funds aside for future uses. Over that hurdle, there are others: The costs of the plan. Flexibility in choosing the investments you retain. The performance of those investments. Restrictions on your entering, departing, or reentering the plan. The commitment you must make to the plan. (Must you contribute every year if you once do it? In what amount?) Restrictions that may prevent you from getting at your money. Penalties (tax and others) that you would incur if you threw in the towel.

It's time once more for further soul-searching to determine how you feel about being separated from your funds for a lifetime, what your guess is as to how much your money will buy you at the take-out window, what your guess is as to what the tax rules will be then, and how committed you are to sacrificing anything today for the unknown tomorrow. These questions are not for a financial planner other than yourself to answer because none of our Ouija boards is any better than yours.

Caution: Ignoring, as I have, state taxes may make these ruminations even more (how shall I say it?) academic. Be sure to check into these possible complications.

With all this on your plate, you should now be able to fill out the table below. Having it handy will help you as you establish your financial defense in Part Three, since it is the base to which you must add as you prepare for retirement or guard against possible disability and other needs.

BENEFITS

Type	Cost to You	Benefits Provided	Other Provisions

For your years of loyal service in completing this table, I hereby bestow on you the Order of the Golden Watch.

CHAPTER SIXTEEN

A STRAITJACKET UNDONE

This time I'm going to be up-front with you. The last time, I led you all the way through the maze before telling you we were working on the preparation of a balance sheet. I don't like being devious. I'd rather be direct. If I had told you we were working on a balance sheet, I feel I would have never gotten you to do it. Now, however, we're old and trusted friends, so I feel more confident that I can get you to do a budget (there's that dirty word) even if I have to tell you right up-front that that's what we're doing.

A budget has a bad aroma. Most people have the impression that it's a straitjacket: that it must be stuck to the side of the refrigerator and that strict adherence to controlling every millicent is mandatory. That's not necessary. You may feel that you don't want to face up to the results of the poor financial management the budget may reflect. That I can comprehend, but not accept. You may not want to put hours into understanding what a budget is, learning about someone else's form or designing your own, and spending endless evenings with your green eyeshade, playing the role of bookkeeper. Those concerns I also can comprehend, but again cannot accept. If you are going to become a financial stalwart, you must face down the beast and time it.

So, what is this thing called a budget? And how should it be used?

A budget is a living document. The numbers you put into it are numbers that cover a specific period—a day or a week if you are paranoid about minutiae, but more typically a month or a year. Unlike your balance sheet, which takes a snapshot of a fixed point in time, your budget encompasses all the numbers reflecting the extended period under investigation. The period may be retrospective of bygone days, or it may be prospective and peer into the future. If you like looking over your shoulder, you'd collect all your figures from that period by reconstructing your past history. Ruffling through your checkbook or peering into old pay stubs or (gulp) scanning last year's income tax return will produce most of the numbers. The rest you can reconstruct using a mild amount of imagination and a filling piece of fudge. Even if you're concerned with projecting the future, you will have to start with the past. That's the best way to begin. Once you've been through the collection routine, you can project from it and add whatever numbers comply with your expectations.

Every budget has three main sections. Care to guess what they are?

So that I don't keep you in suspense any longer, they are (1) the section showing your cash receipts during the period or, to use the technical term for this, your income; (2) the section showing your cash outlays during the period or, to use the technical term for this, your expenses; (3) the section showing your net gain or loss during the period (income exceeding expenses or vice versa) or, to use one more technical term, your budget surplus or deficit. The shorthand label for this last calculation is known as the bottom line. (I know you've heard that term used in many places in many ways. Now you have the source of the phrase.)

I will take a few minutes of your time over the next few chapters to look into each of these sections in moderate detail.

No one can impose a budget form on you that fits all situations. You should construct your own form that works best for you. By doing that, you will feel more adept at the process and won't have to struggle to learn the offbeat ideas of a loony who doesn't know your circumstances. Only gelatin fits into every mold.

I'll share with you my own column headings, and you can feel free to use them or reject them as you see fit (see page 67).

We'll fill in the columns over the next few chapters. I show you the headings now just to show you the direction we'll head in.

Once you've got your form, how do you use your budget and what should it do for you?

As I've pointed out, you can use your budget historically or prospectively. If you use it to look back in anger, you'd make up

BUDGET

Name of Item   *Dollar Amount*   *% of Total Income*
(Income or Outlay)

the categories of items you're concerned with (more on this in the next two chapters) and fit your figures into those categories.

Voilà! You've got a record of your seedy past. Right off, that does something for you. It tells you what you've been able to do with what funds over a given period. It reinforces your fears that things have been out of control, or better yet, it gives you the peace of mind of knowing you are indeed in control and faring well. Thus, it is educational, and educational mainly for you.

Part of that education permits you to see where it (the money) comes from and where it goes. The obvious next question is: Is that where you want to get it and where you want to spend it? If not, or if you're simply searching to discover where change is possible or sensible, you can see that, too.

If you want to use this document on a futuristic basis, you can use it to control your financial affairs. What I do is to prepare my budget for the next month near the end of the current month. Let's say we're in July, and I'm looking ahead to August. About July 24, I'll prepare a projection of my expected income and expenses for August. I'll use my figures from last July to do my projections if I have them, and if I don't, I'll use a one-twelfth estimate of my yearly figures. I'll use the "Dollar Amount" column and head it "Projected Dollar Amount." The "% of Total Income" column will become the "Actual Dollar Amount" column. At the time I do my projections, I will use the "Projected Dollar Amount" column. As we enter August, I will pencil in the numbers as they actually occur into the "Actual Dollar Amount" column. Near the end of August, I will do a projected budget for September (and on and on ad infinitum). At the end of August, I will add up all my actual numbers for August and compare them with my projections. This will tell me how well—or how poorly— I'm doing. It will put me in charge and keep me in charge. I will rest easy knowing I'm doing fine, or knowing what I have to do to get control. After only a few months of this, I will have nothing to be concerned about. I will be the master of my money.

While I'm thinking of it, I should say that none of your budget numbers have to be fined tuned to the penny, let alone to the nickel, dime or even dollar. You want an approximation, not an audited report. You want comfortable ranges that give you some leeway, not a dictatorial monster that puts you under pressure.

Finally, like the balance sheet, the budget gives you a basis for comparing one period's experience with another's. How are you doing?

Was that as bad as you thought? Doesn't this put that filthy word "budget" into a different light?

CHAPTER SEVENTEEN

WHAT COMES IN . . .

. . . should be shown in the income portion of your budget.
That is, most of the things comprising your income should be
shown there. But not everything.

I am stingy as to what I'll let you show as income. The things I
will permit you to list are those items that you can count on.
Regularly. Repeatedly. Continuously. You get what I'm driving
at. Include in your income those items that you are sure of, those
that you know will most likely be there on an ongoing basis.
Nothing is really for sure, so it's a matter of probabilities. Include
the income items which are most likely to repeat themselves. This
is especially true if you are using your budget for projections or
for control purposes. History, some genius once said, after all, is
history. He was awarded the Nobel Prize for statemanship.

Disregard the non-repetitive items of income, or those you feel
you can count on as most likely not to continue.

What are samples of income sources that fall into each of these
categories?

On the inclusion side, things like salary, fees, interest, dividends, rental income if you're a real estate tycoon, receipts from
the Social Security system if you're getting benefits, any pension
receipts if you're retired, trust income paid to you if you're so
lucky, alimony, child support, continuing contractual payments—
whatever is countable and most likely to continue. On the exclusion side, I would omit things like the occasional profit you
may make from your investment activities, the birthday gift you
receive from your Aunt Matilda, winnings in the office football
pool or the weekly poker game or in the lottery, a windfall in-

heritance, a sporadic burst of bucks tossed in your direction. To be truthful, the delineation between the two groups is arbitrary. You can be as arbitrary as I, and you have the tremendous advantage over me in that you know your situation. Carve up your income into those two camps, and list on your budget those that you feel safe with. The others can be parked in the back of your brain for mental fodder to give you a sense of additional security or to cushion your caution.

The categories you choose to use in the income section of your budge. are those that most neatly fit your situation and desires. If you need a line for your salary or your self-employment income, that is very likely to be your best starting place because that is very likely to be the most important to you. If you need a line for hush-money, fine, put it in.

I would list the included items in the order of their sizes, the largest numbers first. By doing this, you will have the focus on the largest source of your income and the other items will dwindle in importance as you run your eye down the remaining listings.

The total of the included items represents your total income for budgetary purposes.

Try my little table on for size:

INCOME

Name of Item	Dollar Amount	% of Total Income
Salary	$1,000	100
Interest	50	—
Dividend	4	—
Total income	$1,054	100

The interest and dividend income are shown as zero percentages in the last column because they are so small in relation to the total income and because rounding them off to the nearest 1 percent of $1,054 results in zero. The method for finding what percentage one of your own categories represents in relation to your total income is: Divide the gross (total) income into the item you are considering and multiply by 100. You will come up with its percentage value.

By any stretch of logic, you cannot work out the percentages until you arrive at the individual numbers comprising your income and tote them up. Where did I get the numbers? From my paycheck or checking account statement as to the payroll information. (And before you ask, I use the total pay—or self-employment income—I receive or expect to receive, before taxes or any other deductions for anything.) The interest and dividend figures can come from a number of sources. The quickest is from my balance sheet. (Recall that we put the indicated annual income an asset is expected to produce in parentheses directly after the asset's name? Now you know why.) Other figures for your income section can be gotten from those same sources.

Try your hand at your own income section before I wipe it out in the next chapter.

CHAPTER EIGHTEEN

... MUST GO OUT

Now you see it, now you don't. It disappears just as quickly as you can pull it in. Oh, how many times I have heard that complaint. Be reassured. We're all in the same fix. Somehow, no matter what we take in, the more we need and the more we have to lay out. This is the layout chapter.

As with your income, the categories of cash outlays (or cash disbursements—"expenses" is not appropriate because not all of these items will be expenses, although each of them will require a cash outlay) are free-form for you to develop. Again, they should match your own situation and your own needs. I tend to establish them in broad-brush sweeps unless I really am interested in what I spend for a specific item or unless I have to force myself to kick a habit. If I want to know or control what I spend for my morning newspapers, then that vice will find its way into a separate line in the outlay portion of my budget. Beyond the curiosity and control aspects, broad categories should do it for you.

Once you have the categories, list them in the order of the degree of control you have over the expenditures. Those disbursements over which you have the least control head the list, those over which you have more control follow in the order in which you believe you have control over them, and at the tail end come those outlays which are most manageable or most discretionary—they're there because you want them to be. I will not pass judgment on your spending habits. You're the only one who can. If you're really upset with yourself, I'm certain you'll do something about it.

Conceptually, here is the way I'd organize the cash outlay portion of my budget.

OUTLAYS

Name of Item	Dollar Amount	% of Total Income
Taxes		
Federal		
State		
Soc. Sec.		
Total		
Withheld		
Insurances		
Other		
Total		
Housing		
Rent/Mortgage		
Insurance		
Utilities		
Total		
Weekly cash		
Programmed savings		
Discretionary		
Clothes		
Furnishings		
Car		
Entertainment		
Vacation		
On and on		
Total		
Total outlays		

Let me repeat a few things before going forward. The categories of expenditures are those that fit you. Once you label them, they should be listed in the order which reflects your degree of control over them. The place to enter such things as expenses relating to self-employment income or rental income is the category I call "Withheld." Not that they are withheld, but that's about the right location for them in the pecking order. The dollar amounts come from your records (checkbook, tax return, pay stubs, bills, backs of envelopes, whatever system you use). The percentage figures for the last column are derived in the same old manner: divide the total of your income into the number on the line you are calculating and multiply by 100. This will tell you what percentage of your total income is going for that item of expenditure. By the way, you see from my collection of categories why I said this section should not be called expenses. Taxes, for example, may be expenses but we tend not to think of them in that way. Programmed savings, if any, are not literally an expense.

This is a good place to try to defend myself and my priorities. What I have tried to do in this listing is exactly what I suggested you should do with your outlays—rank them in order of the degree of control you have over them. Taxes, and by this I mean income-related taxes as opposed to real estate taxes or other types of taxes, are items most of us have some, but only some, control over. They head the ranking. The withheld items (or, for you self-employeds or real estate investors, those expenditures related to the production of income) come next. They offer some choice and some latitude, but pay something toward them we must. Housing is a necessity. (This book is chock-full of those brilliant perceptions.) Yes, we can control the severity of the costs if we can control our emotions or if we can disregard the stew we already find ourselves in. But try not paying our landlord rent under your lease, or worse still, not paying your beady-eyed mortgage lender.

The line for "Weekly cash" is my attempt at giving myself an allowance and some freedom from controlling the specifics it includes. I will give myself, for instance, $100 a week for spending money to cover such things as food, gasoline for the scooter, the morning papers, haircuts, subway tokens, dry cleaning, laundry, and similar expenditures. I lump these items together because I don't want to watch my pennies on each one. If I did, I'd break out the one I'd like to see under the microscope. I give myself this weekly allowance by cashing a check for it. If I find the allowance is not enough, I'll increase my allowance. If I have a regular overage, I'll take a pay cut. (In allowance terms only, of course.)

The "Programmed savings" line deserves a few remarks. It's that old cliché, "Pay yourself before paying . . ." I like to build-in such a category in the middle rather than at the end of the cash outlays. Building it in gives me/you a club to put something away on a regular basis. And putting it in the middle assures that there will be something to put away rather than taking what's not left.

Programmed savings is a tough term to define. It should represent some kind of continuing, formal (written or mentally committed, it doesn't matter) program under which you regularly put something aside. It can include the cookie jar approach, the mattress approach, an IRA or Keogh plan, one of those other employee benefit plans I've mentioned, or an investment program you handle on your own. I am not plumping for the banking institutions. I am plugging the idea of regular accumulation and investment. To be used for whatever your heart desires (or your spouse permits).

Guidelines on what percentage of your total income should fall into each category would be helpful, you say? Indeed they would. They are, unfortunately, non-existent. Sure, you can get surveys showing that families who make between $25,000 and $26,999 spend 32.7 percent of their total income on shoe polish. So what? Should you? Can I, or anyone other than you, tell you what you should be spending on shoe polish? No. If you have a fetish about mirror-glazed shoes, it's up to you to find the money for it.

Having said all that, I will pick out a few categories to give you some ranges of what you can expect or not expect. The categories are income-related taxes, housing costs, and programmed savings.

Do not be surprised if you find that as much as 30–40 percent of your total income goes for income-related taxes. I am not saying this is acceptable. I am saying I am used to seeing these kinds of results. Cut them we must. And cut them we shall. (In passing, this percentage, whatever it is, is not—I repeat, not—your tax bracket. It is the proportion of your total income that goes for income-related taxes.)

Housing costs have gotten out of range. In the very old days, you could figure that if you spent 25 percent of your total income on housing you'd be okay. Now, if you can pay for your housing with that percentage you're in great shape. I have seen numbers going as high as 50 percent to cover housing costs. Again, I am not saying such a proportion is acceptable, just that I've seen it and am not surprised by it. The real limitation on housing costs is your banker. Currently, he has two gauges. One says that your housing costs (rent or principal and interest on your mortgage, real estate taxes and—for some bankers—the premium on your homeowner's insurance) should not exceed 26–28 percent of your total income. His second gauge says that those costs plus any payments you must make on other longer-term obligations (usually defined as those having more than nine months left to pay on them) cannot exceed 33–36 percent of your total income. Those definitions and ranges may vary somewhat from banker to banker. Due to the pressure of inflation over the last several years, the ranges have been reaching higher.

The percentage appropriate for your programmed savings is clouded by another issue. Some financiers use your total income as the measuring stick, and some use your disposable income (total income less income-related taxes) as the measuring stick. The numbers I have seen indicate that, on average, we as a population are saving about 5 percent of our disposable income. If you use total income as your measure, that 5 percent would be a higher number and, therefore, result in more savings. I would push for all I could get. Even at the lower 5 percent, we, as a nation, are usually at the lowest level of savings in comparison with all other Western countries. (I know, with taxes taking about a third of your income and housing taking about a third, you have only one-third left for everything else. That's why we have to cut taxes and kill inflation.)

Not much in the way of guidelines, I know. But what good are guidelines anyway when you're starving?

May I ask you now to confront your own disbursements and make up your own cash outlay section?

CHAPTER NINETEEN

THE BOTTOM LINE

Income less cash outlays equals, we fervently hope, a positive number. This number is the amount by which you have improved (or expect to improve) your net worth during the period covered by the budget we are reviewing. (Your net worth may also be improved by the programmed savings you have done or plan to do. It may also be improved by appreciating investments or things like gifts or inheritances that may not flow through your budget.) This surplus in past periods (plus those items I just mentioned in the parentheses, plus any use of borrowed money) is what has been used to accumulate the assets you have shown on your balance sheet. That is the relationship of your budget to your balance sheet. The surplus of a period gets added to your assets and is used to accumulate assets over consecutive periods.

If, instead of a budget surplus, you show a budget deficit, this may mean that you are not saving as much as you think in what you show as programmed savings, or that you are chewing into your previously accumulated capital. In either case, corrective action is necessary.

Whether you are out to wipe out a deficit or to increase your surplus, the choices available to you are the same. You can either increase your income, cut your taxes, or cut your other cash outlays. There are no other choices.

Increased income can come from working harder or longer (a higher-paying job, moonlighting, putting your spouse to work). Since this is not a book on career counseling and since I have no credentials in that field, I'll skip over it. Increased income can also result from a wiser investment program, and on that one I will have quite a bit to say in Part Four.

Saving taxes can result from any one of several steps, and I'll make some suggestions in the next two chapters. Preview: Nearly every one of them involves an investment decision.

Cutting expenditures is a subject I won't touch for fear of offending you. In preparing your budget, you've seen your offenses. Who am I to step forward and pronounce that your shoe polish commitment is too strong? You can deal with your own fetishes, and you can see where you can cut back. Just how determined are you?"

CHAPTER TWENTY

IF LINE 19 EXCEEDS LINE 84—YOU'RE IN TROUBLE

You've got it. The subject is taxes.

But this is going to be unlike any other tax discussion you've ever attended. I won't promise to leave out every one of the indecipherable buzz words or machinations, but I will promise to make most of it friendly, and I hope even understandable.

First, get the notion of fairness out of your brain. When it comes to taxes, there's nothing fair about it. The tax code represents some legislative body's (Congress or those bums in the statehouse—forgive my severity, I'm from Massachusetts) determination of what social policy should be embodied in the taxation program. The deliberators sit in a fog, perched atop a hill, bending to and fro with their perceptions of what the electorate wants. Since the boys (and girls) want to maintain their windy positions, they must accurately read the mood of the voting public. Give 'em what they want, they say. Or—the next best thing— what we think they want. So, believing that the passage of laws can cure any ill or dictate any policy, they pass laws. Those laws reflect the phone calls and letters that you and I direct at them, the consensus of opinions elucidated in the press and the polls and, if you want to measure the strongest pulse of the populace, the strength of lobbyists. Is this too cynical for you? Sorry. That's the way I see it.

I wanted to give you the right slant on this tax business before we got started trying to explain some of the substance. Let's just say that the tax codes represent someone's determination of what social policy should be as seen from afar and founded on what may be extraneous considerations. That is the allegedly logical foundation of what I will try to explain—but will not defend as fair, equitable, symmetrical, or necessarily rational.

In this chapter I'll explore the fundamentals. In the next chapter, I'll concentrate on applying some of the ideas.

Ere we go too far too fast, I must ask you to wrap your phalanges around your most recent Federal income tax return (and your state return, and, if you should be so unfortunate, your city return as well), pull the nasty thing back from oblivion and cast your hateful eyes over its gray matter. (I shall exclude specific consideration of any state and city taxes for several reasons. Some states and cities don't have them. They are diverse where they do exist. Many of them use the same structure or terminology as the Feds or simply tax on a flat percentage of the Federal tax. You can lay your local returns next to your Federal returns and follow this diatribe in tandem.) Warm up to your return. Think of it not as an enemy, but as numbers fitted into tiny boxes bearing little relationship to your emotions or your efforts. Get familiar with its layout and scan its language and your numbers that wind their way toward the final blow: the total tax due.

If you're any kind of a student at all, you will have discovered that there is a huge gap between the total cash income you received for the year under review and something called taxable income. (To assist you, I'll give you a clue: Taxable income usually falls around line 36 or 37. But the form designers insert and delete so many things every year that I don't want to disclose the exact location. The adventure of seeking it out will add to your excitement.) It is on this thing called taxable income that your actual tax is computed. Since this is so, and since I've said that your taxable income is less than your actual income, need I tell you what the object of the contest will be? Why, natch, to reduce your taxable income.

Reducing your taxable income is the objective because not only will you pay less tax on a lower taxable income, but the tax *rate* is graduated so that the lower your taxable income, the lower the rate that is imposed. To provide you with some relief, the highest tax rate you can pay is 50 percent. Sleep peacefully knowing that no matter how great your success, you can always keep 50 cents out of every dollar. (Ignoring those state and local fellas.)

Now, the tough question: How do you reduce your taxable income?

There are three ways: (1) Reduce your income. (You heard

me.) (2) Increase your write-offs. (3) Take some steps in your personal life which will lower the boom. (In many ways, maybe.) More on these alternatives in the next chapter. Here I want to lead you through the architecture of the form to get you comfortable with its structure.

I can boil down the lines, tables, schedules and murky instructions to a non-threatening three-step process without losing much in the way of substance. Take my hand and let's pick up some of their jargon on our journey. This discussion will show you what the concepts are rather than take you on a line-by-line analysis of the quagmire. My thought is, if you can comprehend the structure, more likely than not you will be able to realize what it s about and how to use it to your benefit.

Step One

We start with a list of your cash income. You should have already done this list for me in preparing your budget. Contrary to my attitude in the budget arena, I take an expensive view of what to list. I like to start with all your income from all sources. Forget that we're looking at a tax return. Forget any concern as to what is, and what is not, taxable. List all your income. All of it. Thus:

TOTAL INCOME

Source	Dollar Amount
Gross earnings	
Interest	
Dividends	
Proceeds on sale of GM share	
Proceeds on sale of condominium	
Social Security benefits	
Payment on a loan you made to me	
Total income	$_____

End of step one. Was that tough? Hardly.

Note what I've done. I've taken a liberal reading of what constitutes your income. I did it because this is what the revenue code does. It is broad in defining the types of income that would be subject to tax. You can presume that any income you receive is going to be considered income for tax purposes. It is, unless there is a specific denial by the code. For conceptual purposes, it's good to think this way.

Step Two

This step will require a few more words to handle, but it won't be rough going. It is here that we chop away at your total income to reduce it to the taxable income portion. We encounter several different types of reductions that accomplish the chopping. Although the terminology differs for each of the several types of reduction, the result is the same—the reduction of your total income to your taxable income.

First, some kinds of income are not considered to be income. (Do you like that style of doublethink?) The one that jumps to mind immediately is the interest paid to you by your municipal bond holdings. Municipal bonds are IOUs issued by states or any political subdivision thereof. Some Supreme Court justice—I believe it was John Marshall—ruled in the early days of the Republic that the power to tax is the power to destroy (little did he know what that would mean to us personally!) and, therefore, interest paid on municipal obligations could not be taxed by the Feds (and vice versa). To this very moment, that concept has been a monument of legal precedent. You have just learned about the world's sole, absolute, permanent tax shelter. Interest from municipals is tax-free. Totally, for all time. Never, ever, will it be taxed. This is the only tax shelter that can make this statement.

The second kind of income we can view as non-income is some dividend income paid by some corporations. In general, the first $100 of dividends received by each and every taxpayer is not taxed. Dividends are distributions of some portion of a corporation's earnings, and the theory is that we should be induced into investing in corporate America (at least, minimally).

Next, we come to a large income/nonincome item. When you sell an asset (such as your share of General Motors or your condominium), any profit you make or any loss you incur has certain tax ramifications. The asset in question must be what's known as a capital asset. In loose terms, this is any asset you own which is not used in your trade or business as part of your inventory. It is important to measure the length of time you hold on to such a capital asset before you sell it. (Recall our notation on your balance sheet of the acquisition date of those assets whose values could fluctuate. This is the reason for that notation.) If you hold a capital asset for six months or less, any profit would be fully taxable. If you held it for more than six months, only 40 percent of the profit would be subject to tax and the remaining 60 percent could be tax-free. (The "could" is in there because there is a provision in the tax law which might make some part of this nontaxable portion taxable. The label is: the alternative minimum tax. I will not lead you into that labyrinth here, but you should be aware of it, and all of my discussions of the tax consequences of these profits are qualified by that possibility.) The usual jargon refers to anything held six months or less as short-term, and anything held longer than six months as long-term.

What if you have a capital loss? Any loss, short- or long-term, can be used to offset any (short or long) gain. So we should be talking about net losses—those losses that exceed any gains. The loss can be used to reduce any other taxable income you received. You cannot offset more than $3,000 of other taxable income in any one year. The amount you don't use in the current year can be carried over to following years and applied against any gains or against other taxable income. If the loss is short-term, you can offset other income on a dollar-for-dollar basis. If it is long-term, every dollar of loss will buy you only 50 cents of write-offs against other taxable income.

How do you tell if you have a profit or a loss? Check the selling price on your GM share or on your condominium. Subtract from it the selling costs. Then subtract from it the tax cost figure we discussed in Chapter 10. The difference is your gain or loss for tax purposes. One major point here is that you get back a larger bundle of dollars than you may be taxed on, and that's what got me off on this discourse in the first place. In doing so, I've planted the seeds of an investment discussion I will come back to again and again. One of the major reasons for investing is to make a profit which qualifies for long-term capital gains taxation to achieve the favorable tax-free results I've just mentioned. (Alternatively, if you face a loss, short is better than long for the reasons cited.)

To finish off this catchall of income items which are not considered to be income items, take from my table above the Social Security benefits and the loan repayment. Why? 'Cause they're not considered to be "income." I can understand that the loan repayment is not. (After all, you were taxed on the money you received when you received it and before you could lend it.) But the Social Security disturbs me. Before the revolution strikes, I'm not saying Social Security should be taxable. I want to postulate a hypothesis for you to consider. When are you more likely to be in a higher tax bracket, when you are earning or when you are yearning? OK, now let me introduce a fact or two. In the earning years, when you're paying in those Social Security "contributions" do you realize that there is no allowance for the payment of those taxes on your tax return? In effect, you never see those dollars. You have them withheld from your paycheck before you receive it. You are paying a tax on a tax. And you are doing it at a time when you are almost certain to be in a higher tax bracket. The final fillip: The Social Security tax (forget this "contribution" baloney) has been the fastest rising of all taxes over the last two decades. Would it not be better to skip the tax on that tax in your earning years when you're in a higher tax bracket and then tax it in your retirement years when your income will be lower and so, too, should be your tax bracket? Logic fails again. The rules bend the other way. (There is, however, some movement in this direction. Starting in 1984, the Feds may tax a portion of your Social Security if your income less certain exclusions exceeds certain minimums. That's the "taxable" side. Keep whistling for the deductibility.)

From looking at these income items which are not, we switch to another through-the-looking-glass concept—expenditures you make which wipe away the income you received on a dollar-for-dollar basis. These are actually expenditures, but they are treated as reductions of your income.

I'll cite two sets of expenditures which are related to the production of income. First are all the current expenses you incur to produce your self-employment income. Second are the operating expenses you incur to produce rental income from investment real estate. Each of these sets of expenses comes off the top taxwise and leaves you with a net income that is subject to tax. (Somewhat analogous to these types of expenses are those expenses you incur in connection with your job which your employer does not reimburse you for. These, too, come off your income.)

Then there's the whole grab bag of miscellaneous outlays that have the same effect. Everything from the payment of alimony (which, by the way, is taxable income to the recipient) to the amounts you contribute to your IRA, Keogh, 401k or 403b plan. There are others. Inspect your 1040 (the official form number by which the Federal income tax return is known) and give special attention to the "adjustments" part on the front of it. For this grab bag contains what are labeled "adjustments to income." Those that are allowed are specifically laid out both by the code and on the front of the form. Wander not from those strictures, or your adjustment will be disallowed.

The result of reducing your total income by those expenses which are legitimate tax expenses and by knocking off the bites of non-income income will put you face-to-face with an entry dubbed "Adjusted Gross Income." This concept has little practical value and is a convenient midway stopping point at the bottom of the front page of your Federal form. Honestly, it has some limited value. It is used in one or two later calculations to determine the exact amount of certain expenses you can write off (medical expenses, for instance), or to determine your actual tax by alternative formulas designed to stick you as good as possible.

To put this wordiness into tabular form with the hope that it will strike you as being clear, I offer this:

REDUCTIONS OF YOUR TOTAL INCOME

Some Types of Income	Dollar Amount
Interest on municipals	
Dividend exclusion	
Non-taxable portion of long-term capital gain or net capital loss	
Social Security receipts	
Loan repayment	

Some Types of Expenses	
Expenses related to self-employment income	(cont.)

Expenses related to rental income
Expenses related to your job which are
  not reimbursed by your employer
Alimony payments
Retirement plan contributions
  Total reductions of your income $_____

Subtracting the total reductions from your total income produces your Adjusted Gross Income. Sigh. Don't be a smart aleck just yet. We've got to get through another group of offsets. These are banded together under the heading "Deductions." Once again, they are specifically defined by the tax code writers and, unless an item falls into a defined category, it's a no-no as far as deductibility is concerned. (The reductions of your total income that I've brought you through have more value to you. They offset, dollar for dollar, your income. Deductions are tolled against something called the zero bracket amount—which I'll get to shortly —and have value when they exceed that amount.) Take a peek at your Schedule A (if you have one) of your tax return and you'll get some clues as to what is and what isn't acceptable as a deduction. I won't list them all here, I will demonstrate how they work.

I make a list of the expenses I've incurred which qualify as deductions (see top of next page).

The total possible deductions must be compared to that fictitious figure called the zero bracket amount. If you're old enough to remember the days when the New York Giants played their home games in Yankee Stadium, you'll remember this concept as the standard deduction. Some lyrical code-concocter got carried awry and changed the phraseology from "Standard Deduction" to "Zero Bracket Amount," or for those of us in the know, simply the ZBA. The theory behind the ZBA is that each taxpayer is entitled to an allowance in recognition of the mere fact that he or she exists. The legislators decide what our "allowance" should be and then throw us a sop for our survival. As I write this book, the guys and gals have determined that if I were a taxpayer who filed as a single person I would need $2,300 to get by, and if I were a married taxpayer filing a return with my spouse I would need $3,400 to survive. Man, are those amounts adequate for survival in the late twentieth century. What a bonanza! Why, those num-

POSSIBLE DEDUCTIONS

Item	Dollar Amount
Medical expenses exceeding 5% of my adjusted gross income	
My state (and city) income tax	
Real estate taxes on property I use personally	
Interest I paid on loans or credit accounts	
Charitable gifts	
Tax or investment expenses	
Other permissible deductions	
Total possible deductions	$_____

bers probably represent a month's lunch money for the setters of the thresholds. Good news follows. In future years these amounts will be ballooned along with inflation. There will be no need to worry then—unless you'd have trouble getting by on that amount currently.

If your total possible deductions do not exceed the ZBA, you are free to deduct none of them. If they do, you are free to deduct the amount which exceeds the ZBA. Put another way, your possible deductions toll against the ZBA, and they have no deductible value unless they exceed the ZBA. The label stuck to the amount of the excess deductions is, of all things, "Excess Itemized Deductions." Itemized in the sense that you must list them. Deductions in the sense that they reduce your taxable income. Excess in the sense that they exceed your ZBA. No need to worry about losing your ZBA, for that amount is allowed for in the tax rate schedules we'll get to shortly.

Here's what it looks like in tabular form:

If the ZBA is higher than the total possible deductions, this difference would be a goose egg. A difference greater than a goose egg means you have something to reduce further your income for tax purposes. That is a good thing.

Please bear with me through one more paragraph.

There is a further sop presented to us mortals. It is labeled

EXCESS ITEMIZED DEDUCTIONS

Total Possible Deductions	$_____
Deduct the appropriate Zero Bracket Amount	$_____
The difference (excess) is	$_____

"Exemptions." An exemption is another bone flipped to us in recognition of our existence. Depending on the state of our being, we may ring the brass bell with one or more of these. We get one for me, one for my spouse if we both sign the same return, one for each dependent I possess, one more if I or my signing spouse is over 65, and yet another if I or my signing spouse is blind (but not deaf or otherwise physically or mentally handicapped). Ring up a grand for each exemption. Again, good news. This $1,000 per will rise with inflation in succeeding years.

With the completion of that paragraph, I can now complete the second step in my tax calculation course. From Adjusted Gross Income subtract your Excess Itemized Deductions (if any) and your Exemptions. Believe it or not, the resulting number is your "Taxable Income." And you thought you'd never live to see the light. It is on this figure, as I've cautioned you, that your tax is imposed.

Before leading you to the third and last step, I'd like to review how we got here. In summary form, here's the story:

COMPUTING TAXABLE INCOME

Total up your total income:	$_____	
Reduce it by:		
Income that is not taxed (if any)		$_____
Expenses allowed as adjustments (if any)		$_____
Excess itemized deductions (if any)		$_____
Exemptions		$_____
What remains is your Taxable Income	$_____	

That's all I've been trying to say.

Step Three

Now, to step three, the actual calculation of your tax.

Deep in the bowels of the instruction booklet accompanying your tax forms you must have seen a series of tables headed "Tax Rate Schedules." (No doubt, you have seen others headed "Tax Tables." I am going to ignore this second set because they will tell you your tax but they will not tell you your tax bracket. Knowing your tax bracket is important, as I've suggested, because it is one of the three navigational stars fixing your status in the cosmos. It is also important to know because it is a quick handle on making some investment decisions. More to come.)

There are four different tax rate schedules available for your selection. The one chosen depends primarily upon your family status and, in an occasional situation, on how you choose to file your return. The various tables are for single individuals, for married couples who file the same return, for married couples who choose to go their own ways when it comes to signing a return, and for a special "Head of Household" class, a table aimed at lowering taxes in certain situations. Ye chooses which schedule you fitteth under, and then ye calculates your tax. A modest sample appears on the next page.

Let's assume your taxable income is $32,000. To find your tax on that amount, run down the first column until you find the range that includes that figure. You will find it to be $29,900–$35,199. Running across that line, the table tells you that the tax on the $29,900 is $5,034. On your additional income of $2,100 ($32,000 less $29,900), the tax is 30 percent, or $630. So your total tax is $5,664. And, lo and lo, you are in the 30 percent tax bracket, the percentage figure given in the third column. That is the rate at which each additional dollar of your taxable income will be taxed until you reach the next rung on the tax ladder. In shorthand terms, this translates into saying that for each additional dollar of taxable income, you will pay another 30 cents (until you surpass the $35,199 threshold). That's all there is to it.

Please forgive me for the length of this chapter. There was no way to stop halfway.

For an educational exercise, take your last tax return and work through the numbers shown on it by placing them on my grid.

TAX RATE SCHEDULE

If your taxable income is between	Your tax is	Plus this %	Of the excess over
0 and $3,399	0	—	—
$3,400 and $5,499	0	11	$3,400
$5,500 and $7,599	$231	13	$5,500
$7,600 and $11,899	$504	15	$7,600
$11,900 and $15,999	$1,149	17	$11,900
$16,000 and $20,199	$1,846	19	$16,000
$20,200 and $24,599	$2,644	23	$20,200
$24,600 and $29,899	$3,656	26	$24,600
$29,900 and $35,199	$5,034	30	$29,900
$35,200 and $45,799	$6,624	35	$35,200
$45,800 and $59,999	$10,334	40	$45,800
$60,000 and $85,599	$16,014	44	$60,000
$85,600 and $109,399	$27,278	48	$85,600
$109,400 and above	$38,702	50	$109,400

You will learn a great deal in the process. The resulting tax, calculated my way, will, however, be slightly off from the actual results shown on your return. I did not want to belabor all the intricacies of every nuance of the code. But I did give you the major structural framework, and it will produce a very close approximation of the final result.

CHAPTER TWENTY-ONE

MUNCHING ON YOUR TAX BITE

Well, here we are again, confronting your income tax return. In our last go-round we encountered the gargoyles crowning the architecture of the tax structure, and you learned (I sincerely hope) that the tax you pay is levied on your taxable income (which is quite a bit less than your total cash income). I suggested, and I'll repeat here for your further edification, that you can reduce your taxable income, and thereby reduce your tax, by one (or a combination) of three techniques: (1) Reduce your income. (Stop laughing.) (2) Increase the reductions granted by the Infernal Code. (3) Take some steps in your personal life to shake down your tax bracket.

I'll start with the last of these suggestions because it's the dumbest. Maybe you think the way to beat the tax rap is to get married. That way, you tell me, you can file a joint return (meaning each of you lovesick lonely hearts signs the same return), and that will spread your income over two bodies in the hope that two can pay cheaper than one. Nope. Not true. At least not true when it comes to taxes. As you may recall from my statements in the last chapter, there are four different tax rate schedules. One of these is for married couples who blissfully sign the same return. The effect of applying this schedule is the imposition of a marriage penalty. If each of you had the same income and write-offs and filed separately, the total tax bill for two would be lower than what it is under this schedule. In an effort to avoid this, or to reduce its force, the current law carries an allowance in the adjustments section permitting some portion of the earned income of the spouse with the lower income to go untaxed. Though beneficial, it is not totally amelioratory. There still exists a marriage penalty where each spouse has some income. (And these days, show me a household where that doesn't happen.)

Your next excuse for taking the nuptial vows is that you can get an extra exemption for your spouse. C'mon. Are you in your right mind to tell me that that thousand-buck write-off (even when it is adjusted for inflation) will save you more taxes than it will cost you in new calico dresses or moustache cups or lace curtains? (Wo)man, you are out of touch with reality.

The obvious next resting position is to say that with a spouse come the darling infants. A $1,000 saving for each each year. True again, but ridiculous. Some financial planning types will tell you that the cost of hatching, feeding, swaddling and passing on the collected wisdom of previous generations will run you between $100,000 and $125,000. Better think twice before climaxing your tax planning.

Neither would I recommend rapid aging or blindness as appropriate tax-saving devices.

In brief, when it comes to exemptions, they are nice to have when you want to have them (or fall into them, like the age 65 bit), but don't go out of your path in an attempt to save taxes this way.

On to more fruitful labors.

Some things you do in your personal life do, in fact, reduce your taxes and save you money at the same time. I'll give you a moment to think of some.

Did you think of home ownership? Or charitable giving? Or supporting the medical profession? Or buying books on (or attending classes on) taxes or investments? Each of these involves a permissible deduction which can help build your list of deductions and may get you over the zero-bracket-amount threshold to the wonderful land of excess itemized deductions.

Hold on for a minute. I do not mean to say you should squander your funds for any of these noble causes. I am saying that if you want to (or must) incur these outlays, you might as well look to doing it in a tax-sensible manner. Take them one by one. If you're interested in taxes or investments (and who isn't?), and you're a taxpayer or investor (and who isn't?), save your receipts for your book purchases or classes in the hope that you can use them for write-offs. Give up reading fiction and going to calligraphy courses. Spend all of your budgeted book or class money on the subjects of taxes and investments, and you'll be helping yourself financially. You also may meet a member of the other sex who is better prepared to feather the next. See what rub-off advantages good tax planning can provide?

Medical expenses, in many cases, are not controllable. Where they are, however, you may be able to use them to your tax advantage. In every case, keep a record of them as you progress through the year. Where the services are elective, you can juggle them from year to year if you think about using the election not only for your purposes but also for tax purposes.

When it comes to charities, there may be a smarter way to give. You probably noticed that your elementary school solicitation carries a plea to give securities to it along with, or in lieu of, your gift of cash. There is a tax reason for this as well as the additional shot at another plea. It's cheaper to give appreciated property than it is to give hard cash. If you give cash, you must give a dollar to deduct a dollar. If you give property that has moved up substantially in value since the date you acquired it, you can deduct the value of the property as of the date you give it rather than the paltry sum you paid for it. Isn't that a nice bonus?

Note the humanitarian nature of these last two examples. In one, you're allowed to deduct the amount of your medical expenses (if they exceed 5 percent of your adjusted gross income). In the other, you can deduct your gifts to charities. In both instances, you can deduct them only if they, plus all your other deductions, exceed your zero bracket amount. Now, how's that for humanitarianism? Dare you call me cynical?

With home ownership we come to something more tangible for you to bite into. In nearly every case, it is the presence of home ownership that will carry you over the threshold of the zero bracket amount. Your real estate tax alone may do the job or get you most of the distance. If you are a borrower, the interest on your mortgage will certainly get you over the threshhold. (I stick to my earlier position. You do not go out and borrow simply to save taxes.) By having either or both deductions show up on your tax return, you are gaining tax-wise from an expense that you would have to face anyway. (I read a learned book once where the author told me housing was a necessity.) If you need to live somewhere, why not do it on the most favorable tax method? To repeat, if I may: Homeownership gives you a deduction for your real estate taxes and your mortage interest (if any), and either or both of these is frequently enough to get you over the barrier of the zero bracket amount, thereby opening the floodgates of deductibility for all those annoying little items that you incur anyway (state and local income taxes, medical expenses, charitable gifts, those books and classes of yours that I mentioned earlier, and a raft of others) that never amounted to a sufficiently large hill of beans to benefit you. Now that you're over the ZBA, tote 'em up like madness. But don't go out looking for them just to deduct them. Where you need something, it's wise to do it in a tax-favored fashion. But you must need it.

Further write-offs?

One that comes to mind is the allowance given each year for the purchase of equipment that is used in a trade or business. The idea began with your ability to write off the first $5,000 of money you spent for such equipment in one swoop of the pen rather than having to spread it out as a deduction over five or ten years. That number continues to inch up to higher plateaus, so the appeal is stronger.

One of the real advantages of investing in real estate is your ability to write off an amount each year that doesn't require the outlay of actual dollars (beyond those you used in the purchase). This lovely is dubbed depreciation, and I'll show you its allures in a later chapter.

Don't overlook those retirement plans. You achieve the tax breaks. But you also stuff it away for later enjoyment. And you must take care of yourself. The Social Security system is held together by mirrors, chewing gum and your vote. Your employer's plan is having difficulty. Add to your 401k, 403b, IRA and Keogh (if it fits). (You can add to your thrift plan, too, but this won't give you a current-year write-off.) In each of these, the question of tax savings is clear. The real question is whether you can afford it on a budgetary basis or whether the lure of tax savings leaves you cold without cash.

Time for a demonstration. I'll use an IRA since this is the most universally applicable of the list. You have earned income of at least $2,000, and you want to put it into an IRA. Your motive is to be applauded. You put it away. You're in the 30 percent tax bracket. You save $600 on your tax bill. (Or, looking at it in another way, the Feds haxe contributed $600 of your $2,000 by letting you put it there instead of into their coffers.) And you have contributed the additional $1,400. Indeed, you have set aside the entire $2,000. If you hadn't done it, your tax bill would have been $600 higher. Now that you've done it, you're net out of pocket $1,400. My question: Can you afford it?

I'll give you another tip. If you're going to contribute to an IRA (or Keogh), do it as early in the year as you can. That way, the money can work for you for a longer period and—equally attractive—the money that money earns wlil not be taxed to you during the year.

To conclude, I want to go back to cutting your income. Of course, I'm saying that tongue-in-cheek. But not entirely. You can cut your income (meaning the income that is recognized for tax purposes) by taking advantage of the rewards offered by municipal bonds, the $100 dividend exclusion, or the long-term capital gain treatment. You may get some income that is protected from taxation by the use of a tax-sheltered investment. (More on these in the last part of the book.) Under each of these methods, you would be switching the source of your income to a more tax-favored source.

You may want to reduce your income by shifting its receipt into different pockets or different years. The different years approach is easier to focus on first. Take a United States Treasury Bill, for example. This is a debt of the U. S. Treasury that must be paid in a year or less from the time the Treasury takes on its obligation. If you buy one, you are lending money to the government. It will, presumably, repay you at the appointed time. These bills are sold at a discount from their face value. When they mature, you are paid the face value. The use of them as investments is appealing for their safety and liquidity and also for the potential they offer of shifting taxable income from one year to the next by buying bills which mature next year. The interest is taxed on maturity, so depending on where you are in a year, you may defer the taxation into the next year.

Another way of deferring income into later periods is by selling an asset on an installment timetable. Let's say I sell you my condominium. We agree on a price of $50,000. I don't want to receive all of that this year because I paid only $10,000 for it and I'll have a large capital gain. We agree you'll give me $20,000 now, $20,000 next year, and the remaining $10,000 two years from now. Focusing solely on the taxation of this transaction, I will not be taxed on the remaining $30,000 of the sale price until the next two years. I will be taxed only on the gain reflected in the $20,000 I receive this year.

Switching income into different pockets entangles other individuals or other entities with your affairs. If you have a child, to cite one simple example, and you set up a separate account for junior, the income the funds in that account earn may be taxed either to junior or to the account depending on what type of an account you establish and what the provisions of the account are. (If you use any of that income to relieve yourself of any of your legal obligations to junior, you're going to be taxed. So use them for frivolities such as dancing lessons or a boat or an education. But not for food, shelter or clothing.) Or, to cite one further example, you may have a parent or two who needs your aid. Throw some assets into another pocket and let the income be used for mom or dad's assistance, and they, not you, will be taxed on the income. In each of these situations, we have used the money for what we wanted to use it for, but we have deflected it away from your own taxation. As I said up front, some tax planning requires competent technical help. I'm just whetting your appetite.

Notice anything common to most of these ideas? Nearly every one has to do with some aspect of investing. Pure and simple: When it comes to saving taxes, it almost always comes to investment decisions. Too bad, but that's the way the world is. Them that has can find ways to have more.

A corollary of this last point: The least desirable manner in which to get income is by the sweat of the brow. That kind of money is all taxable (except for what we can shelter by spending it for allowable expenses or putting it aside for retirement.) We can't move it around into more favored sources of income. And, worse still, we must get out there every day and perform our magic or it doesn't come rolling in. How sad.

My intent in this and the preceding chapter has been to give you a sufficient backdrop of understanding to start coping, and to stimulate your imagination by giving you a smattering of ideas that deserve attention. My intent was not to rehash the tortured language of the tax code and peer into its hidden secrets.

Need further help? If Scribner's will forgive me, I buy the annual edition of J. K. Lasser's *Your Income Tax*, which is published by another company. You can't miss it. It's cover is a gaudy yellow and red. Its pages are filled with facts and suggestions in language you won't find intimidating (although it's a far cry from mine). There is a modest cost associated with acquiring the paperback (tax-deductible). If you prefer, you can get a similar tome from the IRS for zero dollars. But there are few helpful tips there, and we all know whence they flow.

If printed materials don't get you all the way, you can turn to the professionals in the legal and accounting fields. When you do, you will have a good understanding of what they're talking about.

A couple more helpful tips from me before I close:

1. There are some quick ways to get a quick fix on the tax sequences of something you contemplate. Knowing your tax bracket, you can estimate those consequences just as I did with the IRA above. Say you're in the 30 percent tax bracket. If you "spend" something (as I did with the IRA contribution), the expenditure will save you 30 percent of its cost in taxes. If you add more income, you will net from that additional income (after Federal tax) 70 cents on the dollar. As you know, these are approximations, but they are quick.

2. Another approximation: Long-term capital gains. Because only 40 percent of the gain is included in your taxable income and because you know your tax bracket, you can estimate the amount of the gain you will pay in taxes. Thus 40 percent of the gain is included, and you're in the 30 percent tax bracket; 30 percent of 40 percent equals 12 percent: you will pay 12 percent of the gain in tax. (If you want to put a lid on this estimate, I mean estimate the maximum tax you will face, multiply 40 percent—the amount of the gain subject to taxation—by the maximum tax rate of 50 percent, and you get 20 percent. This is the maximum portion of the total gain that you will have to pay in taxes. This last statement is qualified by the reservation I made in the previous chapter concerning the alternative minimum tax: it depends on the size of the gain—if it's a whopper, you may pay more.)

You can use my skeleton format from the previous chapter to keep track of your tax information as a recordkeeping device. Or you can use it to estimate your tax for the year (and some of us have to do that once every quarter). Or you can use it to do projections of your tax to review the consequences of an act if you made certain changes. Those are the uses I get out of the form.

CHAPTER TWENTY-TWO

THERE YOU HAVE IT

Alas! We know who you are financially. We've fixed your status by having you put together the three financial statements containing the pertinent information of what you're worth, what your income is, and what your tax bracket is. These statements, your balance sheet, budget, and Federal income tax form, give a financial planner most of the grist for his or her mill. The collection and organization of these data is the highest hurdle you'll have to leap. Add to them the footnotes to your balance sheet (fringe benefits) as I did, the information about your insurance coverage (still to come except for that which is job-related), and the provisions of your estate plan (in the next part), and not only do we see where you are but we also see what you've got to work with, what changes are possible, what the costs of those changes might be in taxes or lost income or lost liquidity or more expenses, where the gaps are in terms of missing safeguards, and where opportunities might lie. At our present stage, we know enough about you to determine whether you're a candidate worth dealing with. What do you say? Do you see enough from your financial statements to make it worthwhile to do something for you? If so—and I'm positive the answer is positive—let's try to get the safeguards in place and then get on with the profit-making.

PART THREE

DEFENSE

CHAPTER TWENTY-THREE

SAFETY FIRST

Protection is the byword of this part. I want to ensure that you are protected from life's uncertainties and upsets, so that your financial well-being is not torn apart by something that you could have protected yourself against.

When I mention the word protection what crosses your mind?

Why, of course, insurance. That's what insurance is all about—protecting you, your assets and your income against loss. We'll discuss the various types of insurance, measure you up for needs (no, not from a salesperson's perspective) and show you some money-saving devices.

But protection goes well beyond your insurance needs. It confront other topics such as the manner in which you own your property, the provisions of your will (and any trusts you may have), the levy gouged from your estate by taxes, and the necessity of having some funds available that you can grab in a moment of dire need. The first three of these I include in what I refer to as your estate plan. Notice that it has some lifetime aspects to it—namely, ownership arrangements of your assets—in addition to considerations of how your property is to be distributed upon your death and the taxes that your estate might have to pay. The final chapter in this part looks at the adequacy of your emergency funds. These funds are the first line of defense when money is needed in a hurry and when you also do not want to disturb your sound investment program.

Don't step off that curb till we get your defenses in order.

CHAPTER TWENTY-FOUR

CATASTROPHIC COMFORT

It is comforting to know that when disaster strikes, your insurance company will be there exuding warmth, understanding, and cash. Or at least cash, which in turn supplies the warmth and understanding. For you or me, a disaster in our daily lives can be the end of the show. But for these institutions, it's an everyday occurrence and their line of business. You want to use them as a source of indemnification when a loss occurs. A gigantic loss. One that you are unable to handle yourself and should not think of handling.

From their side, insurance companies whir up their computers, tickle their actuaries, and formulate a rate card that will ensure them a profit even though they must withstand a multitude of claims every working hour for calamities that have struck their policyholders. They are in the business of pooling risks, measuring what their underwriters determine those risks to be, charging for their acceptance of the risk, and mathematically coming out ahead on having fewer or less expensive claims made against them than they have taken on. That's how they're able to build massive skyscrapers, advertise on television, and have hordes of money to invest in real estate, bonds and stocks. Spreading the risk is their livelihood, and spreading it in a way that is profitable for them is what keeps them in business.

From our side, we must be glad they're there. If they weren't, we on an individual basis would not be able to withstand the loss. Small losses we could and should withstand, but the big ticket blot outs are for the heavies.

The selection of every kind of insurance coverage should depend on your responses to these issues:

- What is the nature of the risk you are seeking protection against?
- How likely is that risk to occur?
- If it does occur, what is the size of the potential loss you face?
- What does it cost you to transfer that risk to someone else?
- Does that someone else have the financial muscle to withstand your claim?
- What kind of "service" does he provide?

By thinking through your insurance needs in those terms, you will purchase the right kinds of coverage.

Protection from risk. Conceptually, that's what insurance—any kind of insurance—is. I know their terms get far more complicated than this. But if you think of it in these terms, you will know what you need insurance for, what type and amounts seem reasonable and whether or not you believe you're getting your money's worth.

To define the types of risks and the types of insurance coverage available to meet them, I'll give you a short chart. These are the standard kinds of risks most of us face in our humdrum existence, and they will help you survey your own needs. In the next three chapters, I will test the adequacy of your coverage.

I will do my best to help you decide which of those types of coverage and how much you need in the next three chapters.

I will also make some suggestions on how you can save some money on your insurance premiums. Here are some comments that apply to all types of insurance: it does pay to shop. I know that's an old saw, but there are ways to save. The insurance business is trendy, just like everything else. You will find fads. You will find companies that determine they want to write a certain amount of certain kinds of insurance, and they go out of their way to do it. They may have determined that their losses were not as great as they thought or that a certain line of business is profitable or that by writing a certain line of insurance

INSURANCE

Type of Risk	*Type of Coverage*
Damage to, or caused by, your car	Automobile insurance
Damage to your tangible personal property or real estate	Homeowner's insurance
Damage to another's property or physical harm to another caused by you	Liability insurance
Medical expenses	Health insurance
Loss of ability to earn income	Disability insurance
Loss of life	Life insurance

they can bring in more business in other areas. The short of it is that competition among companies has its rewards for you and me.

In general, there are two major types of insurance company, the stock company and the mutual company. The stock company is owned by its shareholders, and any profits the company makes are supposed to go to them. The mutual company is owned by its policyholders, and any profits the company makes are supposed to go to them. This is in theory. In theory, also, the premium you pay a stock company may be higher than the net premium (net after your share of the profits) you pay a mutual company. Generally, these days there is not much difference, if any, in the premiums between the two, but in specific instances there may be some.

It is more costly to purchase an individual policy on your own than it is to obtain coverage under a group policy. However, cost is not everything. You can tailor your own policy to your own needs. You have more control over it. But the benefits provided may be wider in the group policy.

Piggybacking may save you money. If, for example, you have a basic policy provided by your employer, you can pick up extra coverage on top of that on your own. This will be far less costly than if you bought the basic coverage and then went the entire route on your own.

Another suggestion: Technically, there may be a difference between an agent and a broker. An agent works for, and sells exclusively, the products of one or more specific insurers. A broker is hired by you to search for the best deal he or she can find on your behalf. This line has gotten quite fuzzy. There may be no practical difference, for in the end you must trust and believe the person you are dealing with. (But, regardless of their titles, it may benefit you to get proposals on an identical package from two different sources. Even if you're just "testing" or shopping, it won't hurt.)

Deciding on the types and amounts of insurance packages you need is not so difficult. Shopping for and comparing competitive policies is something else. To the suggestions I've just provided and those I will provide, I point you in the direction of *Consumer Reports*. That magazine does eye-opening comparisons of the policies offered by nearly every company writing each risk.

CHAPTER TWENTY-FIVE

CHARIOT, CHATEAU
AND CHATTELS

Amidst the splendor of your accumulated possessions, have you dared think of what your world would be like if you were relieved of them? Lift your eager eyes from these pages if you can and survey your environs. From the roof shielding you from the elements to the soft seat under your arrears to the Rembrandt gracing the wall, the diamond solitaire perched on the oilcloth-covered breakfast table, the chariot nestled at curbside, the *Sea Witch* bobbing at dockside at your secret Shangri-La—what would you do without them? Poof! There goes a lifetime collection of tangible belongings. And then? Well, you'd replace them, hopefully with goods of equal caliber. That's where insurance comes into this serene setting.

Total loss of your assets by disaster or theft is only one of the risks that can befall them. Damage to them is just as likely, if not more likely. And there is a further risk you run. The Rembrandt may tear itself away from the plaster and bop someone on the noggin. Or a feeble guest might miss the edge of your Persian rug and go sprawling onto its texture, never to regain the composure of his or her ankle. Or your chariot may impose a dimple on the sleek front fender of another motorist's magnificent Monza, or worse still, your failure to guide your chariot properly may impact the unprotected torso of a pedestrian or another operator of a six-thousand-horsepower machine. The latter types of error, in which you do harm to another or to another's property, is the reason for purchasing liability insurance. The former ones, in which your property is somehow damaged, destroyed, or purloined, is the reason for purchasing property (sometimes called casualty) insurance. We will study the types of property you may own, the kinds of disasters that can occur, and the main points you should consider in acquiring your insurance.

Let's begin with your chariot. You may refer to it as your scooter (as I did earlier), your toy, or (in search of a nickname) "Tiger Eye." In every instance our focus is on that heap of metal, plastic, and glass that cost you about fifteen grand. I've already suggested the kinds of evil you can perform with the behemoth. Ruin it, have it heisted, see it vandalized, hurt someone, kiss another monster, or whack a structure. Your worries are to repair or replace your jalopy or to provide recompense to the owner of the other property or to or on behalf of the injured party.

How do you measure your potential losses? In terms of the value of your chariot, in terms of the value of the unknown property you may collide with, and in terms of the loss you dump on to another human. The potential size of the loss to your machine is measurable. That is, its present value. That value you can obtain from your reliable car dealer or a little item known as a Blue Book that should be in his hands or in the hands of a banker who is used to giving loans on jalopies. Presumably, you can afford the small nicks and knocks that may befall your car, so you can take a moderately high deductible, say, $250 or $500. That says you're willing to absorb the first pummeling up to that amount in each transaction harmful to your car, but that anything that reaches into the higher realms you will hand on to your partner, the insurer. The higher the deductible, the lower your premium, and the savings may be substantial. Further, your chariot may be older, approaching the age of senility. In that instance, you may not want to pay for the "comprehensive" coverage—coverage that deals with things like loss from fire or vandalism. The cost of the coverage may be more costly than the value of your car. In short, take a good, objective look at the age and value of Tiger Eye, insure for its value, up the deductible to your breaking point and chop the extraneous coverages that are too costly or that you don't need. (One of the silliest of this last type is coverage for towing. If your car goes bango, the insurer will pay you $25 for towing it. I know you can afford that.)

When it comes to measuring how much is enough for damage to other people's property or to others, the going gets tougher. What's your driving record look like? How congested is your locale? What's the cost of new chariots? Pick a good, high number and relax. On the liability to people issue, I would take the highest amount your insurer will sell you. Claims for personal injury or death are out of sight and getting more so. Any lawyer worth his or her license who brings suit on behalf of a plaintiff usually works on a contingency fee basis promising him or her 30-40 percent of any recovery. You know they're not going to sue for $300 when they can sue for $2 mill. Put the armor on and shore up the defenses.

Items of tangible personal property that surround you, other than your car, usually have no great market value. This I have suggested way back in my chapter on your assets. But they do have value for you. You need them. You would suffer an enormous loss if you had to replace them. Look at the oilcloth, the spreading chair beneath you, the sofa, your snuggies, the Revereware in the kitchen, the boob-tube, every stitch adorning your abode. It adds up. These items can be stolen, destroyed or damaged. My measuring stick is what it would cost you to replace them if they were totally gone. Estimate. That will be close enough. Unless you happen to have a Rembrandt, or a sable coat, or superlative silverware, or a diamond bauble. In these (and a few other) cases you will need an appraisal from a qualified appraiser.

One trend now underway in the insurance industry is the willingness to insure these belongings on a replacement value basis rather than an "actual cash value" basis (an estimation of what the property is worth today figured by taking your cost and reducing it by the years of wear and tear). This, as I say, is a trend. Not all companies do it. Not all companies do it for all types of property. (Their fear is, and has been, that it's too easy for your old TV set to disappear so you can replace it with a new one at their expense. This may be a valid concern in some cases, but knowing you, I know they have no reason to be so concerned.) Where available, my preference is for replacement value. That will make you whole in the event of loss. It will eliminate the haggle of settling on a claim's value. And it will cost you a higher premium. Again, lift the deductible. Or buy a "floater"—coverage only on that piece of property that you are most concerned with.

This coverage may be wrapped up in a broader type of policy referred to as a homeowner's policy or it may be purchased separately. If it's in a homeowner's policy, the policy carries with it other kinds of protection. For example, it also includes coverage for property of others that is on your premises, and it includes liability protection against claims made by that feeble stumbler within your premises. Generally, it is cheaper to buy the several pieces wrapped together in one package than to buy them separately. (Here, once more, I would obtain the maximum amount of liability coverage the company will sell you. For the same reasons I just mentioned.)

Don't be deceived by the name "homeowner's" policy. These policies apply to you whether you're a tenant, a condominium or cooperative owner, or an actual homeowner. If you're a renter, they may be called homeowner-tenant policies. They insure your personal property and include the other types of coverage I've just given you examples of. They do not insure any loss to real estate for, of course, you own none. The beginning point for measuring your premium is the value you (or you and your appraiser) place on your belongings. From there, the cost goes up or down with the add-ons you want (like increasing the liability protection) and the deductibles. A homeowner's policy for a condominium or cooperative owner is very nearly identical to a homeowner's policy for a renter. Once again, there is no real estate to insure. (That's what I said, no real estate to insure. The real estate is insured by the entire association of owners. That policy is referred to as a master policy and its premium is usually part of the monthly maintenance charge.) The only additional things such an owner may choose to insure are improvements or fixtures within his or her unit. This is done under the homeowner's policy. And there may be policy options available which deal with the special problems created by these types of ownership. Some of these options I feel are extremely wise to purchase —for example, those protecting you against liability claims made against the association which could result in a further assessment against you.

Before saying a few more words about a homeowner's policy for a true homeowner, I'd like to say a few more words about liability insurance. Not that I'm paranoid about it. I recognize the nature of today's litigious society, the potential size of the claims, and the desire to protect what's yours. In addition to the maximum coverages available to you on your automobile and homeowner's policies, you can for a very few dollars pick up a policy dubbed an umbrella or excess liability policy. It comes in and pays off your obligation above the level of your underlying policies. It is available to you in multiples of million-dollar chunks. If you want to protect your assets (and, in some states, your income) against attack by horrendous claimants, this coverage is a bargain.

Back to the homeowner's policy. The remaining comments I have to make relate to the amount of insurance you carry and the definition of "value." To be consistent, I believe you should insure for replacement value rather than actual cash value. This type of insurance is not available on all types of homes in all locations. For instance, your home may be a sixteenth-century baronial with hand-carved balustrades and purple-paned windows. Not really replaceable. Or it may be in a neighborhood which has not maintained its values so that the replacement cost is far in excess of any realistic market value. These are legitimate reasons for the insurer to refuse to write replacement cost average. But, where available, I would prefer it.

How do you get a quick estimate of what the replacement cost of your home is and therefore know what to insure it for?

Forget about the value of the land and the foundation. These are supposed to be indestructible by anything short of a nuclear attack. Take the overall outside dimensions of your home and multiply those numbers to obtain a square-footage figure. (For instance, if your home is 20 feet wide and 50 feet long, it contains 1,000 square feet of living space.) Find out from a local contractor or mortgage lender what the approximate building cost is today to rebuild a home like yours. Let's assume it's $50 a square foot. Multiply the square footage by the square-footage cost to rebuild, and you get $50,000. That should be your insured value.

You should also obtain an inflation endorsement. This increases the amount of coverage on an agreed method during the life of the policy. It will automatically keep your coverage more or less in tune with current costs.

My experience has been that most people are woefully underinsured on their personal property and home. This underinsurance results from inattention and rapid inflationary increases. Please make sure you're not one of these unfortunates. Pull out your policies, list them here and do the calculations I've suggested to see that your coverage is up to snuff. We'll both be happier.

EVALUATING COVERAGE

Type of Property	Value to Protect	Amount of Coverage	Premium
Car(s)			
Personal property			
Valuables			
Real estate			
Liability			

CHAPTER TWENTY-SIX

SICKNESS
NEED NOT BE TERMINAL

Woe is you. You've got an advanced stage of that rarest of rare diseases, misbegotten money-worrisitis. Dreadful. Destructive. Its symptoms are a furrowed brow and an aching head founded on a fear of financial havoc resulting from illness or accident punctuated by deeper fears of uncontrollable drains on family finances and ultimate bankruptcy. (Take two aspirins and get a good night's sleep.)

As you can see, there are two sides to these symptoms—one, the phenomenal expenses of illness, and the other, the possibility of a wipeout of one's assets. They are interrelated. If you look to insure against incurring expenses relating to medical needs, you will, by having an adequate type and amount of such insurance, protect your own assets. There is another type of asset, however, that this insurance will not protect. It is very probably your largest asset. Any guesses as to what it might be? Why, natch, your earning power. Take the total number of your working years, multiply that number by your average annual earned income (or even your current earned income), and look at the size of that figure. Now, compare it with the dollar size of any (or all) of your other assets. Surprised? I'm not. It's the protection against the loss of that asset—your earning power—that is the province of disability insurance. (I'll try to be supportive—a vast majority of workers do not have such insurance, do not have it in adequate amounts, or do not consider it critical.)

I will look first at the expense side and then at the lost income side.

On the expense side, I will go all out to promote the maximum coverage you can obtain. Medical expenses can wipe out anyone, and have wiped out quite a few. The trend of rising costs seems to me certain to continue as highly skilled medical professionals become more in demand and more specialized, as new technological advances produce more and more expensive equipment, and as longevity continues to increase.

We can look at protecting you against the incursion of medical expenses in two ways: through preventive means or through curative means. I will not step into the debate about which is superior. Under the preventive approach, you take steps while you are well to prevent illness or to reduce its costs if sickness should occur. Under the curative approach, assistance steps in when needed.

Health maintenance organizations (HMOs) are designed to work on the preventive side. They are made available to you usually through your employer or through a group you belong to. It is now a Federal requirement that any employer who has twenty-five or more employees and an HMO nearby must offer the option of using the HMO to its employees. Because of this, and because of the increasing number of HMOs, there is no doubt they will be growing in popularity. They offer, for a set premium, everything from regular checkups to health care when needed. There are many different types of plans, but they are all targeted to the same objective—to get to you before something happens so that it will not happen or, if it does happen, so that the cost of the cure may be substantially reduced.

Plans other than HMOs offer coverage of, or reimbursement for, expenses actually incurred by you when you get sick or need medical attention. These usually involve some kind of insurance plan. The insurance may be provided by a quasi-government organization such as Blue Cross-Blue Shield or by a private insurance company. Some employers do what is called self-insure some of their risks. This, translated from the poetic language of the industry, really means the employer has no insurance—he has determined it is cheaper to shoulder the actual costs if care is needed than it is to pay the premium.

In any event, there are three levels of expense coverage to consider: basic, major or master, and catastrophic. I'd go for all three. Basic coverage carves out those kinds of minimal expenses that barely scratch the surface of your skin in a moment of need. The next level up, major coverage, will carry you most of the way unless you have a long, drawn-out problem. Catastrophic coverage will put some kind of very high dollar limit on the amount of coverage the insurer will provide during your lifetime, or it may in fact carry no dollar limitation. Because all plans and all policies differ, I cannot give you examples of specific types of coverage or specific types of inclusions and exclusions. But conceptually, these coverages work as I suggest.

Health and medical insurance is one area in which you can piggyback on what your employer provides, if it's less than catastrophic coverage. Maybe he offers optional added coverage, or maybe you can get additional layers of coverage through a group you belong to. Even if you must go into the marketplace on your own, by having some coverage in place through your employer you can save premium dollars. In essence, by picking up over a certain threshold, the effect is as if you had a high deductible. These remarks also apply relative to disability coverage.

Unlike health insurance, disability insurance is not for everyone. Notice, please, that at this point I have stopped "selling" insurance. Some sort of casualty, liability, and medical insurance is mandatory for nearly everyone. But other kinds are not. Their purchase depends much more on personal factors. In the case of disability insurance, the key factor is your dependence on your earned income, for this type of insurance is intended to replace your lost earnings—that is, income you lose because you are unable to work due to illness or the results of an accident.

How dependent are you on your earned income? We must go through a four-step process to find out.

First, fill out my table below showing what your income would be if you were unable to work:

NON-EARNING INCOME

Source of Income	Dollar Amount
Interest	
Dividends	
Rental income	
Other unearned sources	
Total income	$_____

These numbers come from the budget you prepared for me. In effect, they take all your budgeted income numbers except your earnings. (While I'm thinking of it, if you are married, and if your spouse works, you should go through this exercise twice— once for each of you, to see what would happen if a spouse's earnings were not forthcoming.)

Next, we must add in any income you expect from governmental programs (such as worker's compensation or Social Security), employer plans (such as salary continuation) or insurance sources (such as those provided by your employer or those you obtained on your own).

INSURANCE INCOME

Type of Benefit	Dollar Amount
Governmental program	
Employer plan	
Insurance	
Total benefits	$_____

Add the total income and the total benefits and that's the cash you should have available to you to support your life-style. Guess what we must do now. Yep. Look at the expenses. From your budget you can cull all those expenses which you expect to continue. You can add to them any additional expenses you may incur because of your disability—supplies, custodial care, domestic help. These will give you a total of your expenses should you become unable to work.

EXPENSES

Type of Expense	Dollar Amount
Ongoing	
Additional	
Total expenses	$_____

Subtract the total expenses from the total funds you will have available, and you will find out whether you are adequately protected against lost earning power or not.

What we have here is simply another form of projected budget. We have peered ahead to a time when, due to disability, you may

not be capable of earning any income. We have used your existing budget as a starting point, taking your current income and
your current expenses from it and adding any other income or
expected expenses to see where they left you. Unless you're fully
protected, I would be concerned. There may be a way to make
up the gap through the use of investments or switching assets
around to produce more, or possibly you're aware of some inheritances that might help. But I want you to be fully protected on
an income basis. Any gap should be closed by insurance.

Tread carefully when it comes to estimating your income taxes
for this future situation. Any insurance proceeds you receive that
your employer paid for will be fully taxable (as will be any salary
continuation plan). All other insurance proceeds will be tax-free.

In the world of disability insurance, there are Cadillacs and
there are non-Chevrolets just as there are in other fields. Here are
some things to bear in mind in reviewing your insurance needs
and protection:

- The elimination period. How long before you start receiving benefits? The longer you wait, the lower the premium.
Policies provide anywhere from a zero-day wait to one year's
wait. Normally, 60 or 90 days makes sense.

- The benefit period. How long does the policy pay? The
longer the better, preferably to age 65 if the disability results from illness and for life if the disability results from an
accident.

- The benefit the policy pays. Most policies will not pay
over a certain percentage of your earnings at the time you
take out the policy (or at the time you become disabled).
This limit may be as low as 50 or 60 percent of your earnings. I've already explained the theory behind this. Will the
benefit go up as your earnings go up while you are working?
Will it go up with inflation after you become disabled?

- The premium you pay. Relate it to the benefits you may
get and make a seat-of-the-pants judgment on whether or
not it seems fair. Ladies, look out: your premiums will be
higher than those of a male of the same age. It is not discrimination, it's just that you have a longer life expectancy.

- The guaranteed non-cancellability and renewability of the policy. The insurer must be required to renew the policy each year for the same premium as long as you choose to renew it. This renewal cannot be dependent on the state of your health.

- The definition of total disability. Does the policy pay if you cannot do your job? Or merely a job for which you are reasonably suited? In other words, is the definition of disability suitably broad to protect you or will you lose your benefit if you retain some competency to do some totally menial task? Is the definition so restrictive that the benefits will be paid only if you get hit by a butterfly while doing a tightrope act? What about partial disability? Can you get something if your earning power is reduced but not completely eliminated?

Weighing these factors will tell you what kind of policy you own.

Take time to make out another of my informational tables using your policies and programs.

PERSONAL PROTECTION

Type of Coverage	Benefits Provided	Premium
Medical		
Basic		
Major or master		
Catastrophic		
Disability		
Governmental program		
Employer plan		
Insurance		
Employer		
Group		
Individual		

CHAPTER TWENTY-SEVEN

THE DEATH PENALTY

When you face the final curtain and pass through the pearly gates, who will step forward and meet the financial obligations you leave in your wake? Think warmly of the life insurance companies you have been paying those premiums to over all those years. At a time such as this, those mammoth institutions can be your savior—or at least your heirs' savior.

While I'm in this religious mode, let me add that buying life insurance, quite to the contrary of what insurance salespeople tell you, is not a moral obligation, something you must do to escape commiting a mortal sin. Life insurance is a financial tool, pure and simple, designed to satisfy certain fundamental needs. Unless you have such a need, forget purchasing any of the stuff.

What are some of the potential needs you might have for life insurance?

You might care to provide for dependents who survive you. If you're married, there's your surviving spouse to look out for. Or you may leave younger children who need to be fed and clothed. Or you may have been supporting a parent whose finances have been ravaged by inflation or illness.

You may feel the pressure to cover the costs of private schools, Bulla Bulla Moola Moola colleges, or the august expenses of specialized graduate education for your young-uns. Or there may be some other nut you feel honor-bound to crack.

You may have amassed tons of debts you want to wipe clean from your closing balance sheet. A mortgage on the family manse, a car loan, a personal debt granted to you by a mail-order lender.

You may desire to leave your marvelous estate intact, untouched by the thrusts of administrative expenses and death taxes, and to see those intrusions met by the "free" money emanating from life insurance policies used to pay the piper.

You might want to be a benefactor for your Alma Mommy, the Museum of Refined Arts, a crypt for your pet mockingbird, or a final show of affection for your paramour.

These, in my book, are possible uses for life insurance proceeds. (I will add one that I feel is definitely not: a source for the payment of burial expenses. By the time you have finished paying premiums, you could have paid for the plot six times over. Anyway, if you get cremated and have your ashes scattered, you're looking at a tab of less than $500—and you're not tying up valuable real estate that someone else can use or can develop as a condominium.)

Each of these possible uses for life insurance has a measurable weight or value attached. By adding up the measurements, you can determine how much life insurance is enough. I'll take you through some of the math.

Take the first possibility, the need to support a survivor. Work from your budget. Assume you need $30,000 a year for your survivor to meet his or her ongoing expenses. Do you want to provide this amount in perpetuity or for a limited number of years?

OK, you're generous. You want to have the funds received by your survivor each year forever. The next question you must address is: How much can the life insurance proceeds reasonably be expected to earn from an investment after tax? Let's say you're in the 30 percent tax bracket and that you think a 10 percent return is attainable on an annual investment basis. How much must be invested at 10 percent to leave your survivor $30,000 after incurring a tax of 30 percent of the income? Divide $30,000 (the amount needed by your survivor) by seven percent. (It's 7 percent because the annual investment return of 10 percent which you believe can be attained is reduced by the 30 percent allowance for your tax bracket. That is, 30 percent of 10 is 3, and 10 minus 3 leaves you with a net after-tax return of 7 percent.) You'll get $428,571.42, if my tiny hand-held calculator is correct and if you did your division correctly ($30,000 divided by .07). This means you'll need about $430,000 of life insurance to leave your survivor a fund which, invested at 10 percent and allowing for a 30 percent tax bite, would net him or her $30,000 a year each year forever.

To check our numbers, we can work backwards. Start with the total amount of insurance needed, $428,571.42. Multiply that by 10 percent, the expected annual return. You should get $42,857.14 if you're at all clever. That is the amount of income the full nest egg will produce annually if a 10 percent return is available in the investment arena. From that $42,857.14 there must be subtracted an estimated tax bite of 30 percent; 30 percent times the income equals $12,857.14, which is what the tax collector will take. Subtracting that tax bite from the total income will leave a net of $30,000. Right on the money.

All this has been based on the assumption that you want to leave an inviolate nest egg for your survivor. We have kept the nest egg intact and used it for the production of annual investment income. Sure, the conclusions are iffy. Who knows what your survivor's budget will look like? Maybe he or she won't have to make monthly payments on a mortgage because you're going to allow funds to pay it off. Or maybe his or her expenses will go up or down in your absence. Or perhaps the 10 percent return we estimated may not be available. Or the tax laws may change. All of these are assumptions anyone can make, but no one can guarantee. What we're after is an approximation, a range of comfort levels that will tell us that at least your life insurance coverage is reasonably close to what's needed. For, true to confess, no one knows precisely how much is enough. "Enough" is a matter of what you feel comfortable having. No one can sermonize on what that amount is. I'm giving you gauges.

I can cut the amount of insurance needed to care for your survivor if, instead of looking at the generation of income from a nest egg in perpetuity, we look at providing a lump sum which will be consumed over a certain number of years. Suppose you figure a short number of years' coverage is enough, or you leave a survivor who does indeed have some savvy and can go out and earn some funds (or who will be left with other sources of income, such as investments or inheritances). The money you plan on leaving in life insurance is a backstop. Say your survivor needs that same $30,000 a year, but that you figure you need to provide a cushion for only a maximum of five years. In this case, you can multiply five times $30,000 and figure you need leave only $150,000 in life insurance coverage. Since your survivor will be whittling away at the total proceeds of the insurance, we can forget about income tax on this sum. It is not considered to be "income." (True, any of these funds which are not consumed should be invested and will produce some income which will be subject to tax. But, on the approach we are currently taking, the additional income generated will represent gravy.)

The "extra purpose" measurement is just as easy to figure. What is the purpose? School? How many children for how many years at how much per year? Two kids for four years each at $15,000 a year? Simple multiplication tells you $120,000 will be needed. Want to provide funds so someone can be hired to look after those kids while you work and your spouse isn't available to rear them? How much will you need to pay a caretaker? Take that annual sum and do the math I did above when I was calculating my "in perpetuity" scenario or multiply it by a fixed number of years if your needs will end when your children reach certain ages.

Debts to pay? Total them up.

Death costs? Total them up. (I know you can't do that just yet, but you will be able to estimate them after you read my chapter on estate taxes which is coming up.)

Mommy, museum, mockingbird, or paramour—what to provide for whom is a matter close to the heart, and an issue well beyond my ken. What dollar value would you put on them?

By adding all of these numbers together you will know the grand total of life insurance you should have. Don't panic when you see the total. We're long past the days when a $5,000 life insurance policy was meaningful. This total, as I've said, will give you an approximation of how much life insurance might be adequate.

You can see from the manner in which I approached the estimation of how much life insurance you need that, in effect, I am looking at insurance proceeds as a means of replacing income which is lost because of your disappearance. If you are around to keep earning and accumulating, your insurance needs should be decreasing. Think of it in terms of a seesaw. You start life with your side of the seesaw high off the ground, leaving you vulnerable to a crash should you tumble. The other side of the seesaw is planted solidly on the ground. Put into financial terms, when you are in the air your accumulated assets are zero and your objectives are out of sight. You need something to replace your unavailable income and your unaccumulated assets. As you gain weight and add to your accumulated assets, your seesaw ride will come into more of an equilibrium and your insurance needs will decline. Eventually, when you are obese with assets, you will be solidly grounded, and the need for insurance should disappear entirely. In the terms of the industry, insurance will provide you with an instant estate, meaning you have more of an estate when you die than you had when you were alive. True enough in the early years. But if you take my programmed accumulation plan, you should have an estate—without the instantaneous feature. As your assets build through increased income, wise investments, or family dole, you should need less life insurance.

I must remind you that life insurance is a losing proposition. The only way you can win big is to die early. When you purchase a life insurance policy, you are betting against yourself; you are saying you're not going to make it and you want some compensation if you don't. The more years you pay premiums, the less your "return" and the better the insurance company will love you.

Basically, all life insurance can be divided into two major categories, term insurance and cash value insurance. Each of these two categories has several variations.

Term insurance is similar in concept to the manner in which your automobile insurance works. You pay an annual premium and, barring any disasters, at the end of the year you get nothing back and you pay another annual premium a year later. The premium went to pay for the protection throughout the year. If you had had an accident or, for purposes of our current discussion, had died, there would be recovery under the policy. The company would pay off. If you survive, the premium paid was for the coverage during the year. If you died, your heirs would recover. The premiums charged are based on your sex and your age. The older you are, the higher the premium. Men at the same age as women pay more. (Male life expectancy is shorter.) At any age, for both sexes, term insurance is cheaper than cash value insurance. Or, if you prefer, you can always buy more coverage for the same amount of dollars if you buy term insurance.

I've suggested that you can buy any of several variations of term insurance. The most common is yearly renewable and convertible term. Under this type of coverage, the face amount of the policy you purchase (the dollar amount for which the policy is written) remains the same year after year, but the premium increases each year due to your advancing age and the increasing likelihood that each year may be your last. The policy is renewable in that the company must continue to insure you as long as you keep paying the premiums. The company can cancel the policy only in the event of your non-payment. The policy is convertible in that at any time you choose during the life of the policy, you may convert it into a cash value policy.

A few variations:

- A five-year renewable term. This is the same as an annual policy except that the policy is written for five-year periods instead of one-year periods. The premium is paid annually, but it is the same for each of the five years. In essence, it is an average of the premium that would have been paid at different ages in each of the five years. In the early years, you pay more than normal; in the later years, you pay less.

- A ten-year renewable term. Ditto except read "ten" in place of "five."

- A special come-on. All kinds of new twists are thrown in to sell insurance at lower costs. One example is an annual policy that sets premiums in five-year periods. The first year's premium is exceptionally low (to get the business). The second year's premium is about double the first. The next three years' premiums are the same as the second year's. In the next period, year six's premium is higher than year five's, but lower than the next four. It can be lower still if you can pass a medical examination at that time. And so on, for successive five-year periods.

- Decreasing term. A mirror-image of the annual term policy except that the face amount of the policy goes down each year while the premium stays the same.

Now to the world of *cash value life insurance*. This type of coverage combines the "pure" insurance features we have just been discussing with some form of cash buildup under the policy's provisions. The premium you pay combines a charge for the insurance aspects with a segment that is considered to be a cash savings feature. So much of your premium goes for the insurance, and so much goes toward a cash accumulation.

There are several arguments for purchasing this type of policy. You get a forced savings program, if you do not have the determination to do it on your own. This amount can be obtained by surrendering the policy. There will be (after the first year or two, as with the surrender value) a sum of money you can borrow from the company. This will be on favorable terms, as I remarked a long time ago. These funds accumulate additional funds on a tax-free basis. (At the rate of $3\frac{1}{2}$–4 percent, usually, except for the new so-called universal life policies, which earn competitive rates). The premium will not increase for the life of the policy. The policy is permanent, meaning on the one hand that it will continue to be there as you continue to pay, and on the other that your mental set will be different in that the tendency is to keep these policies in force whereas policyholders having term insurance are more apt to let them lapse. And, finally, your insurance salesperson receives a much higher commission for selling this type policy than for selling term policies. So the pitch will be much more fervent.

I'd like to stimulate your imagination for a moment. Because I want to write this entire book without using a single chart, graph or picture, I'd like to have you do a drawing in your mind. It will be a simple drawing: a rectangle with its long side running from left to right and its short side from top to bottom. It should look like a square-cornered hot-dog lying on its side. Now, draw a line running diagonally from the lower left-hand corner to the top right-hand corner. This splits the rectangle into two triangles. The triangle below the diagonal line is the cash buildup that goes on year after year as you pay your premiums and as the cash earns additional cash. The top triangle is the amount of "risk" the company faces under the policy or, in other words, the amount of protection the policy provides from sources other than your own dollars. Let's say the left-hand vertical line of the rectangle is the face amount of the policy—the total amount the policy will pay on your death. The bottom line of the rectangle is the number of years you have to pay the premiums and also your advancing age from the time your started the policy.

The calculations by the company are such that by the time you reach the age at the far right of the rectangle, the accumulated cash value which came from your own premium payments and the earnings on the cash portions of them will equal the face amount of the policy. The company's risk at that point is a huge zero. Your heirs will receive the face amount of the policy which will be fully covered by the amount of your premium payments plus the accumulations on the cash value portions of them. You understand why I said you win if you die early. If you live (and pay) long enough, your heirs will receive your cash value and none of the company's funds. Neat?

How far out the right line goes depends on the type of cash value policy we're talking about. Again, there are variations:

- A whole life policy. You pay premiums every year throughout your life. The right-hand line of the rectangle may be set at age 90 or 99, depending on the company or the policy. What they would be saying in this case is that if you live to 90 (or 99) and pay the premium each year for that period of time, the cash value of the policy will equal the face amount of the policy.

- Payable to age 65 (65-life). The policy stays in force during your life, but you pay premiums only until you're 65. The premiums are higher because the company collects fewer of them.

- 10-pay or 20-pay life. Same as 65-life except that the premiums are paid over the number of years indicated. Again, the shorter the pay period, the higher the premiums.

- Endowment policies. These require premium payments over a set period of years and promise to pay their face values at the end of a fixed number of years or upon your earlier death. This speeds up the collection of premiums and emphasizes the forced savings aspect of cash value insurance.

Which would I buy? Is there any question?
Term.
If you (or your insurance salesperson) are headstrong about

cash value insurance, a universal life policy offers some favorable features in comparison to the traditional forms of cash value policies. These features are a higher rate of return, more flexibility, a policy more in tune with the times. But it is still cash value insurance and retains the drawbacks of such coverage. (Mainly higher costs.)

Underlying all cash value coverage is the confusion between thinking in terms of life insurance as insurance and thinking of it as an investment. Life insurance is not—repeat, not—an investment. It is protection. It offers replacement coverage for lost earning capacity. It will not make you rich. It may make your heirs rich.

A few definitions before I leave you with an exercise.

Who is the *insured?* The person on whose life the contract is written. On the death of the insured, the policy will pay its face amount (less any oustanding loans, if it is a cash value policy and some part of the cash value has been borrowed).

Who is the policy *owner?* The policy may be owned by the insured or by someone other than the insured. Whoever it is, the owner of the policy has certain rights, such as the right to name the recipient of the policy's proceeds on the insured's death, the right to borrow the cash value if the policy has one, or the right to convert the policy to another form if that option is offered.

Who is the *beneficiary?* I gave the answer away in the preceding paragraph. It is the recipient of the proceeds of the policy on the death of the insured. It may be a person, an institution, the insured's estate, or another named entity.

Who should these people be? Those are decisions you must make, decisions that are vitally important in your planning. I believe I have convinced you that you may have continuing obligations to deal with after your death. If you do, you should be the insured. If you have a spouse at home looking after young children, you might wish to insure your spouse so funds will be available to hire help if he/she should die. If you are dependent on your child for support (or a former spouse for alimony), you may decide to insure the appropriate life. Being the owner of the policy provides total control over it. It also means that the full value of the policy is subject to the owner's estate tax liability. If control is not an issue but estate tax saving is, it may be advantageous for the owner to be someone other than the insured (say, a spouse). The issue of naming a beneficiary also includes some consideration of where you want the money to end up, who has control over it and, possibly, some estate tax questions entangled in the decision. More on these subjects in a later chapter.

To gather all your life insurance information in one place, please complete a schedule like the one below. By doing so, you will see how much coverage and the types of coverage you have. If you are married, complete a separate schedule for each spouse.

LIFE INSURANCE INVENTORY

Insurance Company	Type of Policy	Face Amount	Cash Value	Insured	Bene-ficiary	Owner	Pre-mium

Completion of this schedule will tell you what you have. Total up the face amounts of all your policies and then go through the estimation-of-need process I described early in this chapter. By comparing the two, you will see how comfortably you can rest in peace.

CHAPTER TWENTY-EIGHT

WHAT'S MINE IS MINE

Far too often, the question of who owns what is settled on the basis of emotion or appearance or convenience. I claim to have feelings so I can understand why some enamored lovers choose to put the title to their humble homes in the names of both spouses rather than the one who in fact paid for it. Love has powerful dynamics. Sometimes we hold title to property in cumbersome ways just to let the world know we're decent folks. Why, if I put everything my wife and I own into my name alone, you'd think I was a selfish pig, or worse. It just wouldn't look good. (As if anyone could actually see the situation. To put your mind at ease, I'm not that kind of guy. My wife lets me occupy her condominium, and all I've requested is a corner for my desk and file cabinet, a place to hang my clothes and my head, and an easement to the refrigerator.) Some folks own property in a fashion they believe will be most convenient. For instance, a bank account with a mother's and daughter's name on it so that the daughter can get money if her mother needs it and can't get at it. Commendable indeed. But possibly costly in other ways.

Dare I say that the decision as to how to hold title to property should not be made on considerations of emotion, appearance, or convenience? Of these three, convenience is the one having some influence. But I put that influence low on the list of considerations, and I change the word to expediency. As a practical matter: What is the proper way to own property so that cumbersome barricades need not be overcome? Note, please, that my comments imply that a decision must be made on who owns what, and how. Too many times that decision is made by default. It's too easy to slip into something comfortable, or to slip into something unknowingly. No. In every case of owning an asset, a decision must be made.

Why? Because there are major financial consequences that follow title. You might think that matters of property rights, liability risks, insurance needs and costs, tax consequences, and successive ownership are insignificant. But I do not. I believe they are crucial to the choice.

The structure I use in making a choice on who should own what and how is a four-part mind-jogger involving issues of rights and responsibilities and taxes and considers the circumstances of both life and death. My mind-jogger follows, two key questions with two jogging-parts each.

What are the consequences of owning an asset during one's lifetime?

The two sets of considerations here are the practical aspects of ownership and the income tax ramifications.

The practical aspects of ownership encompass the whole bundle of rights and responsibilities that accompany the ownership of anything. Who controls it? Can it be used? Can it be sold? Can it be given away? Can it be exchanged? Can it be consumed? Can it be used to borrow against? Does it need to be insured? Will the premiums be higher because I own it? Is it subject to claims of creditors? If I'm held liable for any reason, will my assets be unprotected? (Covering your assets is the first rule of survival in any environment.) You get the picture, I'm sure. It's a consideration of all possibilities known to man which go with property ownership.

The tax ramifications of owning property are two-faced, those that sock the owner with additional taxable income and those that offer the joys of tax write-offs. Which does the asset provide and where is it best for those chips to fall?

What are the consequences of owning an asset upon one's death?

As with the living side, there are two sets of considerations: the succession in ownership and the burden of the estate tax.

When one dies, who becomes the owner of the asset? Under different forms of ownership, the answer differs. But the idea is to allow for the next owner(s) to be who you want it to be rather than have it merely happen.

Estate tax implications too frequently wag the dog. It is important to know whether or not owning property in certain ways exposes it to the estate tax levy and, if it does, how much of the value is exposed to the tax. Get ready for this one: there may be circumstances when it is wise to stand tall before the imposer and pay the tax. (Please. Don't crumple the page. My point is simply that the estate tax must be considered in the choice of how to own an asset.)

With that structure as a backdrop, what then are your choices in the boutique of ownership forms, and how do those choices stack up on the structure?

First a list of expanded definitions and then some opinions on the selection process.

Sole Owner, Sole Ownership, or, When Operating a Business, Sole Proprietorship

Hey, man, you're it. The cat's meow. You've got it all. All the rapture. All the misery. No one, other than the law, can tell you what to do with it. (Though others may try.)

Tenants in Common

This implies neither a rental situation nor a common-law jointure. It's a mode of owning property in which two or more owners can divvy up the ownership interest in preselected proportions. Each owner has an undivided interest in the whole. It's not possible to lop off (without court order) what specific segment is mine and what is yours. Say there are two of us who own a piece of real estate together under this handle. Say you own a 70 percent interest, and I own a 30 percent interest. Neither of us can point to the specific part that is ours, but we can both point to the whole and say we own those pieces. (If we want to get ours, we can go to court and ask that the property be sold and get our respective portions of the cash raised from the sale.) During the lives of the owners some rights may be limited and some may not be. For example, either of us can sell our portion. But both of us must sign a mortgage if we want to borrow against it and use the property as collateral for the loan. Income taxwise, we would have the income generated by the real estate and the deductions stemming from it divided according to our respective proportions. On death, my piece would go to my heirs and yours would go to yours. For estate taxes, my share would be taxed and so would yours. Not the best of results in many ways, but appropriate for some situations.

Joint Tenants with the Right of Survivorship—JTWROS—or Simply Joint Owners

As with tenants in common, each joint owner owns an undivided interest in the whole. Again, this interest may be disproportionate or equal. But there is one major difference—on the death of one joint owner, the title passes automatically to the surviving joint owner(s). This automatic succession of ownership is the one key attraction for this type of ownership, and I would say its only attraction. If you think in terms of my four-part structure of decision-making, I'll point out that there are many drawbacks to joint ownership. Start with the lifetime situation. If the asset that is owned jointly is a bank account, either owner (assuming there are two) can withdraw the entire boodle. Fine, if that's what you want. But not so fine if you don't want to take on that risk. If the asset that is owned jointly is a security, both owners must agree to sell it (and sign it) before it can be sold. What if one disagrees? If the asset that is owned jointly is real estate, both owners (as with tenants in common) must sign a mortgage, and if either wants to sell his interest, he may sever the joint ownership arrangement, thereby defeating the automatic succession bonus.

Thus, depending on the type of asset owned by the joint owners, the problems may differ. In regard to income tax consequences, the party tagged with the taxable income or benefiting from the deductions must be identified as the real "owner." Which one is that? Why, the one who paid for it, or, to talk in circles, the one who really owns it. On death, sweetness reigns as to automatic succession. As I've said, this is the primary plus of this approach. But so what? What does it really do for you?

Nothing more than put the asset in the survivor's name(s) without any further ado. But the ado is not cumbersome if it must be addressed in any event. On the estate tax question, there may be difficulties. The current Federal estate tax law presumes that where property is owned jointly between husband and wife, half of the value of the asset is owned by the spouse who dies and half is owned by the surviving spouse. Where the joint ownership is between non-spouses, the presumption is that the deceased party owned all the property and so the entire value is included in that party's estate. The survivor can prove some contribution to the acquisition of the asset, in which case that proportion will be excluded from the estate of the deceased joint owner. The burden of proving contribution is on the survivor, and this is not always easy to do. In applying their estate taxes, many states follow the approach of assuming that the entire value should be taxed to the dead joint owner's estate.

Tenants by the Entirety

A form of ownership available only to husbands and wives and applicable only to the ownership of real estate. Other than for some highly technical refinements, it is identical to joint ownership. This form of ownership is losing favor. You will understand why when I give you some history. The concept came from the old English common law (nothing wrong with that). The idea was that husband and wife were as one, bound together tightly as a unit. But that "one" was the husband. Need I say more about why this form of ownership is losing favor?

Community Property

This is not, in the strictest sense, a way of owning property. It is a consequence of acquiring property during the state of marital bliss. Some states follow old canon law which proclaims that any property coming into the hands of either spouse during marriage is regarded as being owned half by each. Roughly, the idea is to reward each spouse for his or her share of the bargain. I throw the concept in here to give equal time to canon law while recognizing Anglican law.

Custodian under the Uniform Gifts to Minors Act

Legislative wisdom has dictated to the legislatures of every state that they adopt a uniform statute allowing for a simplified method to establish and maintain an account that would benefit minors. Property placed in an account established under this act is considered to be the property of a named minor. The custodian must use it and invest it for the child's benefit. Other than that limitation, the custodian has fairly broad latitude. Naturally there are statutory provisions defining what can and what can't be done, but these are moderately painless. When it comes to income taxes, any income on the funds in the account is taxed to the child as long as the custodian doesn't use account money to relieve himself or herself of any legal obligations (such as the provision of food, clothing and shelter). When the child reaches majority (21 in some states, 18 in others), the assets must be turned over to the child. On the death of the custodian before the minor reaches majority, another must be named and, as long as the custodian is different from the person who contributed the assets, the property will not be included in the estate of the giver.

On the death of the child, the assets are treated as if they were his or hers. The beauty of this approach is its simplicity: no lawyers, little paper work, lots of flexibility. Further advantages come from the savings of having income tax imposed on someone in a lower bracket and the potential estate tax savings. The disadvantages are some inflexibility in operations and, most importantly, the fact that the assets must be turned over to the child upon reaching maturity—who may opt to zoom in a Porsche rather than burn out brainpower in halls of ivy as his or her benefactor might have wished.

Trust

This is a form of ownership I'm going to rave about two chapters hence. It can be applied to a myriad of situations and offers supreme flexibility. A trust can define the uses of assets during your lifetime, it can be used to save income taxes, it can handle title succession on death, and it can save estate taxes. Of course, no trust can do all these things at the same time and not all trusts will achieve all these glorious results. Life would be without challenge if it were otherwise. But to whet your desire, I'll give you some hints. Take the preceding paragraph, where we were dealing with the minor child. If a trust were used instead of a custodian account, more flexibility could be built into the document than the statute permits and the assets would not necessarily go directly to the child at his or her majority. But you must pay a lawyer a fee for the preparation of the trust document.

General Partnership

A general partnership is a relationship put together under the terms of a written agreement in which there are at least two parties, each of whom is a general partner. Each partner has control over the management of the asset and shoulders full responsibility for any losses incurred by the partnership. The written agreement defines the relationship and establishes the working procedures. The partnership files a tax return but pays no income tax itself. The income tax is assessed against the individual partners. The death of a general partner, under most state laws, dissolves the partnership. In that event the partnership's assets must be allotted and the appropriate shares taxed in the estate of the dying partner. This mode of ownership is not attractive to anyone except those who know intimately, and trust implicitly, the person they are entering into partnership with. Show me someone like that, and I'll form a partnership.

Limited Partnership

Like a general partnership, a limited partnership is based on a written document which defines rights, responsibilities, and procedures. To create a limited partnership there must be at least one general partner and at least one limited partner. The general partner is the head honcho. He or she swings for the bundle. He or she manages the asset, is in control of all decisions, stands in the driver's seat. But he or she also faces the possibility of unlimited liability if the asset goes sour or causes harm to third parties. The limited partner has no control, makes no decisions and can lose no more than he or she has invested. This last factor is where the "limited" comes in to the title. The limited partner is a passive investor. Because the partnership pays no income tax itself and because the tax consequences "flow through" or are reflected on the tax returns of the partners, this type of ownership is commonly used in tax shelter deals. The written agreement among the partners not only sets the rights, responsibilities and procedures; it also angles the tax consequences among the partners. On the death of a limited partner, his or her interest usually goes to his or her heirs, but it may be bought back by the partnership. The value of the interest in the partnership is valued for, and is subject to, estate tax. In almost all partnership, there is very limited liquidity for a partnership interest.

Corporation

An entity which the law recognizes as having a life of its own, a corporation has the same property rights as any individual. There may be some restrictions placed on it by its corporate charter, but generally it can do what you and I do. It incurs its own income tax (unless it is of a genre known as a Subchapter S corporation, which is no more than a corporation complying with a segment of the Federal tax code that says a corporation that complies with its requirements will be treated as a partnership for tax purposes). It has a life in perpetuity (unless it goes bust or is merged into another goliath). It faces no estate tax. The major attractions of a corporate form of ownership are the limited liability of its shareholders (you and I can lose no more than our investment in the corporation should it fold or do something equally awful) and its ability to raise money by selling additional shares to build an ever-expanding capital base for the business. In effect, it is a means by which a new person, the corporation, can gather funds greater than any of us can do on our own and dedicate those funds to the growth of a business which benefits more than just one of us. This concept is at the heart of our capitalist system, and I will say more about it in the last part of this book. Of course, any shares you or I may own in the corporation can be owned in any way I've mentioned up to now (including ownership by another corporation) with the same results I've described under each heading.

*

And now for some further opinions on ownership. You've already noticed some preferences, I'm sure.

If you're single, you can own assets in your own name, jointly with another, or under a trust. If your assets are very (and I mean very) minimal or mainly non-liquid, sole ownership may be your best bet. It's uncomplicated. If you'd like someone to have access to your assets, you can give that person a power of attorney. This is a written instrument which can be very broad or very narrow in scope, authorizing your named "attorney" to do what the instrument provides. In some states, the power evaporates if you go loony. In some states, it goes with you when you die. To me, retaining control and avoiding the problems of joint ownership make sole ownership desirable. If convenience is a concern, consider the power of attorney. (I should add that it can be revoked at your pleasure.)

The problems with joint ownership, other than those I've already mentioned, are that you don't really know which joint owner will die first. (Consider, for example, a case in which I own property jointly with my mother and it is assumed she will die first, but I get hit by a moving mastodon.) There may be a double tax of the same property in two estates. (In our example, the entire property is taxed to my estate when I get crushed because my mother has no proof that she contributed anything to its acquisition, and it is taxed again in her estate when she meets her fate.) A further problem is that the distribution of jointly owned property on death is nondiscriminatory in that all of the asset passes to the survivor. (Thus perhaps not providing for my sister who needs it or some portion of it.)

If you have moderate (and I mean moderate) assets and a goodly portion of them are liquid, I lean heavily toward a trust for reasons I will expound on in the chapter after next. (I'm building suspense, as a real thriller should.)

If you're married, my reasoning is identical, especially where both spouses are working or where one is working and the other has an independent source of assets such as gifts or inheritances. The main point is to keep track of assets independently of each other and to stake out which are whose. Why? For estate tax reasons. Tracing the trail of assets through the many generations of changes in those assets is not difficult if good records are kept to show where the money came from and where it went. But without those records, one or the other spouse may get saddled with unwanted results and those deadly presumptions on death.

Here's my solution: separate accounts for each spouse. Perhaps a small joint bank account for convenience which each spouse contributes to in some proportion and uses for operating (but not investment or mortgage payment) purposes. Alternatively, each may have a power of attorney from the other. Keep enough in either the joint account or the individual accounts for emergencies. Investments should be owned individually. Some may be owned jointly if adequate records showing contribution and parentage are kept. If the assets are moderate and fairly liquid, each spouse should use a trust; if not, let them stand in each spouse's own name.

Before departing this fascinating subject, let's regroup the assets you listed for me way back in Chapter 10, where I defined assets. Refer to the list you made at that time and fit the facts into the following schedule. In addition, pick up the life insurance policies you listed in the preceding chapter and list their face values here (less loans, if any) according to who owns them. There are two purposes for this schedule: (1) To gather all the asset information together so that we can refer to it when we talk about estate taxes shortly, and (2) to give you a snapshot of how your asset ownership is allocated. Not that we can do anything with this last matter. There are no firm guidelines, but awareness is worth something.

ASSET OWNERSHIP

Type of Asset	Owned by You	Owned by Spouse	Owned Jointly with Spouse	Owned Jointly with Another	Other
Total of each column	$____	$____	$____	$____	$____

CHAPTER TWENTY-NINE

YOUR PARTING SHOT

Brace yourself. Close your drapes. Put on your black attire. Shape your expression into a morbid mold.

You're now prepared to read about wills.

A will is not a death warrant. It does not seal your fate upon its signing. It is a functional document that serves a distinct purpose. It tells those of us who survive you what you would like to have done with your assets, who should be in charge of the management of your remaining affairs, and what legal niceties you'd like to avail yourself of.

A will controls the disposition of property you own in your own name. It has no effect on property which stands in joint names with the right of survivorship for, as we've just seen, that property passes automatically to the survivor. It has no effect over the payment of life insurance proceeds, which are paid directly to the beneficiary named in the policy. (In some situations the beneficiary may be your estate, in which case your will would control the dollars that come into the estate, but not the policy itself.) And a will has no effect on property held under a trust (although you may establish a trust in your will). To repeat: in purist terms, your will controls only the property which stands in your own name.

The provisions of a will which deal with these assets are referred to as the dispositive provisions. They are the provisions which—you guessed it—dispose of your assets. Feel free to express your wishes. You can dispose of your assets as you desire. Oh, yes, there may be limitations in some states. You may not, to take a nasty example, be able to disinherit your charming spouse.

You may not, to take another nasty one, be able to disinherit your child without saying so in explicit terms. You want to leave me a grand? Leave your silver chalice to the public library? Leave everything you've got to the Society for the Prevention of Dispositions? Leave your estate in trust to be used for the benefit of your mother during her lifetime and, on her death, to be given to your siblings or their children? Fine. Simply say so, and it will be. Express your desires, and someone will carry them out.

That someone is called an executor (executrix, if it's a she). The executor's job consists of gathering all your assets, paying off all your obligations, filing the appropriate forms to get the will established in court and its provisions fulfilled, paying the applicable estate costs and taxes and, ultimately, distributing the remainder of the assets in accordance with your wishes. In short, the job consists of winding down your affairs. The job may be easy or hard depending not so much on the total dollars involved but on the types of assets involved (a family business, something requiring technical knowledge or complex manipulations) or the existence or potential of a family feud.

Who should serve as the executor? I prefer a family member. If you're married, your spouse should serve unless he or she has no common sense or truly is vulnerable to the pleas of passing fancies. If you're single, your parent or your child or your sibling should serve. Of course, you do not stop at naming one executor. You may name coexecutors who serve simultaneously with each other. But I prefer that you name successive executors so one can take over if the previously named executor can't complete or fails to complete the job. My preferences for successors—in order of choice—are another close relative, a friend, a business acquaintance, a lawyer, and a bank or trust company.

Why that order? There are a couple of reasons. I start with a spouse or close family member because he or she should know the most about your affairs and also be someone you're intimate with and trust. Going down the ladder, these factors may be present in lessening degrees. Also, family members may take a lower, nominal, or zero fee. They can decide which attorney to use and when to use him or her. They may want to do some or most of the work themselves (and it can be done.) Once you turn to professionals as executors, they are locked into your estate. There is little chance for change or abolition. The fees may be large. The attention to personal needs or imaginative solutions may be low. Nonetheless, they are, by definition, professionals. Presumably, they've done it before and know the ins and outs. And, in the case of the banks or trust companies, they offer continuity—they'll always be there.

In addition to naming an executor, your will may also name a trustee, if you establish a trust in your will. I'll have more to say about the use of a trust in a will and the selection of a trustee in the next chapter. For now, it's enough to say that a trustee's job is slightly different from an executor's. The executor's job should end about fourteen or fifteen months after your end. The trustee's may go on for years. The skills required may be different. The executor may be required to have common sense, personal knowledge of you, attentiveness to detail, integrity, and some basic business sense. The trustee needs to have these qualities plus others—deeper knowledge of investments and taxes and, perhaps, more business savvy. You can be thinking about who would be an appropriate trustee until we get there in the next chapter.

There is one other person you may choose to name in your will to look after your affairs. This person is called a guardian. The guardian's job is to look after any minor children you may leave. This person should be thought of as a substitute parent. You are looking for a proxy for you. Who would you want to raise your child if you're not around to mold him or her in your own image? You had better think of two or three individuals to name. You can name them as coguardians (if they're physically living in the same place) but should certainly name them as successors to cover any vacuums. And for God's sake (and your child's), talk to those you've selected before you select them. The job you're asking them to do is not an easy one.

The three categories of persons I've just named will administer your estate on your passage. The ability to make this selection and to make dispositive provisions are two of the major functions a will provides.

The third is to avoid some legal snarls. There may be nuances in your state's law that can save your estate money by avoiding unnecessary expenses. For instance, elimination of the requirement that an executor have a guarantor on his bond or that someone (a friend of the judge) be named to look out for the interests of persons "unborn or unascertained." Technical, I know.

But a properly drawn will can avoid such hassles—and save you greenbacks.

Notice that I did not say that the existence of a will would save you estate taxes. The mere existence of a will may not. Certain provisions in a will may. More on this topic a few chapters ahead when I turn you into an estate planner and get you to apply some fundamental planning techniques.

Return with me now to the legal profession. I've mentioned the group once or twice. A lawyer is a necessity when it comes to the preparation of a will. Preferably, you'll hire one who specializes in estate planning. Up-to-the-minute techniques, information and styles are essential. This expertise may be sophisticated. If your affairs are relatively simple, the expense of no more than a few hundred dollars is a good investment. If your affairs are substantial or complicated, the cost may run to a few thousand dollars. But, once more, it's a good investment. I am not speaking of these fees as the cost of only preparing a will. They should cover the development of a total estate plan. Perhaps contrary to your beliefs, estate planning covers more than the preparation of a will and, possibly, a trust. It includes decisions on who should own what property and how, who should be the beneficiary of life insurance policies, what should be done with any work-related benefits you may have, and whether a gift-giving campaign makes sense in your situation. Most of these comments refer to ground we've already covered. You can see that in my understanding, estate planning has both lifetime and death-time considerations. Those considerations, in addition to the drafting of a will and maybe a trust, are what the legal fees should go for.

Whatever fee you pay will be modest in terms of what it can do for you. The savings in complications, the avoidance of unknown legal minefields, and the reduction of estate taxes will more than justify it. From the lawyer's side, however, the fees are modest for another reason. The drafting fees are looked upon as a loss leader. They are endured to get the payoff later in handling the estate. That can be quite lucrative, in some states running to 4 percent or more of the total estate. You can appreciate why I said earlier that you should not name a lawyer as an executor unless you have to. Executor fees may be shopped, negotiated, or nearly eliminated if a lawyer hasn't been built into the will.

The best place to keep a will is in the vault of the lawyer who prepared it. This is for safekeeping purposes only. In this case, possession does not represent 90 percent of the law. On your death, your executor should not be embarrassed to ask for it or to shop or to negotiate fees. The second-best place for safekeeping is in a safety-deposit box. The worst place is in your dresser drawer.

Sign only one copy. Comply with your state's laws on the formalities of execution (so the will will stand up and no one will switch a page on you). Simple changes can be made by the use of a brief codicil which must meet the same execution requirements as your will.

The process of establishing the validity of a will and straightening out the title to property it controls is called probating a will. In some states, there are specialized courts known as probate courts (or family courts or domestic relations courts). Their business is to handle this role and others related to family matters (such as divorce, adoption, name changes, and so forth). Your state's laws determine the proceedings and also the types of ownership interests that must pass through the probate court. Is it property standing in your own name? (This is universally true.) Is it jointly owned property? (To my knowledge, never.) Is it life insurance proceeds? (Usually not, unless payable to your estate.) Is it property held under a trust? (Usually not, unless the trust is created in your will.)

Having plumped hard for your having a will, I should stop momentarily and tell you what happens if you don't have one. First off, the state decides who will receive your property and in what proportions. That who and what will not, as many people believe, be the state. The state will take the property only if there are no heirs of yours to be found anywhere. The decision as to who gets your assets is made by state laws called intestacy (literally, "without a will") statutes. These laws are enacted by the jokers in the state legislature and have been known to change on a regular basis. Distribution is according to the relationships of your remaining heirs to you. Further, you have no choice over who administers your estate. Nor are you able to cut out some of the red tape or to save some costs and some taxes. Those reasons should drive you into your attorney's office pronto.

Knowing that you've learned the lesson of having a will before you met me, I'll ask you to pull it out and read it. Don't be ashamed to say that it's old or that you don't remember what's in it. Read it. It will do us both good.

Does it do what you want it to? Does it take advantage of some of my suggestions? Do you understand it better? Would you like to make changes? If so, get on with it.

Normally, a will should hold up well over a long time before it's called on. The draftsperson should be able to foresee most eventualities. But the monkey remains on your own back to police its propriety. If there are major changes in your circumstances (marriage, divorce, a birth, a death, significant changes in asset levels), you should pull out your will and review it in light of the new circumstances. (Some of them—things like marriage or divorce—will automatically revoke your will in most states.) If, in your general reading you discover there have been substantial changes in estate taxes, you should have your will reviewed by your lawyer. Even without these changes, it would do you well to read that will every three or four years to see that it still represents your wishes. For the theory is, after you're gone, all we have left to go by is what's within the four corners of that document. Sayonara.

CHAPTER THIRTY

EN-TRUST ME

Meet a marvelously flexible, multi-goal-satisfying tool called a trust. A trust is always embodied in a written instrument, either standing alone or hidden in the bowels of a will. There are two main divisions of trusts, and one of these divisions is further subdivided into two parts. The two major divisons are trusts which you create during your lifetime and those that are created in your will when you succumb. The first type is known as a living trust or inter vivos trust (from the Latin, meaning during life, in case you're a scholar). The second type is known as a testamentary trust because it is contained in your "last will and testament." Under the inter vivos banner come revocable trusts (those you can change or, in the vernacular, can revoke, alter, or amend during your lifetime) and—surprise—irrevocable trusts (those that are set in concrete once you establish them; they cannot be changed in any way). Each of these types may have different uses. I'll review some of them for you in a bit.

Each type of trust requires the same ingredients as every other type. Each, as you know, must be in writing. Each must have a trustee (a person or institution which is sometimes called a fiduciary—which means he, she, or it acts always for the benefit of another). The trustee is the manager of the trust assets. Each trust must have some asset held under its terms. (It may be one dollar, $100, $1 million, securities, real estate, tangible property, a copyright, a contract—in other words, any kind of tangible or intangible property—and the property may be added to or reduced.) Each trust must have one or more beneficiaries (those who benefit from the trust), and they may be simultaneous or successive, present or contingent, income or principal, living now or born later. Each trust must have a set period at which it will terminate (next week, in 1999, on the death of someone, on reaching a set objective), and that termination date cannot be so far distant that the property in the trust is effectively tied up in perpetuity. Each trust must set forth the powers, duties, rights, obligations, authority, procedures and other operational factors under which it runs. (For my money, the more flexibility the better.) And each trust must include certain legalisms or the law will get you. (For example, a provision that the trust may be altered, amended or revoked must be present if you want to have a revocable trust, or in some states you'll end up with an ir-revocable trust.)

Those are the common elements. You get the flavor of the flexibility in applications and language already, I'm certain. To demonstrate these points better and to show you some of the vast variety of choices you may have in using a trust, I'll give you a sample of one common application and a few other potential applications. My sample will be one for a married person, but the same holds for a single person except that, obviously, there would be no need to provide benefits for a surviving spouse. (Although you may want to provide benefits for a surviving child, parent, other dependent or "friend.")

I visit the plush offices of my specialist estate planning lawyer and present her with a list of my family members, assets, disposi-tive ideas, and names of desired executors, trustees, and guard-ians (which list will save her wasting time in asking for those items and save me part of her fee). After discussing my goals, I go home and await the receipt of some draft documents from her. I receive them, read them over, conclude they do what I want and I return to her office to execute them. I do execute them, leave the original will and one of the two original trusts with her, and I'm set to go.

The will I have signed is very simple. It leaves a few trinkets to my spouse if she survives me and, if she doesn't, it leaves them to my children to be divided equally. The rest of my assets will be "poured over" (added to the trust I have just established) when I die, to be administered under the trust's terms. I name my spouse as executrix and name a couple of business acquaintances as successor executors. The will is fleshed out with all kinds of legal garbage. The function of the will in this case is to "catch" any property I may own in my own name when I die and add it to the trust property. It is my intention to hold all of my property under the trust so the will offers backup protection for any assets I might have mistakenly forgotten to transfer to the trust.

I transfer all of my assets to the name of the trust. I do this by establishing bank and securities accounts in the name of the trust and by deeding over any real estate I own to the trust. I may make the trust the beneficiary of all life insurance policies I own. In any case, let's assume I have transferred all my assets to the name of the trust.

Under the terms of the trust, I am the original trustee and the beneficiary of the trust. Because I am the trustee and because I have reserved the power to revoke, alter, or amend the trust at any time, I retain total control over the trust's assets. Upon my incompetency, incapacity, or death, the trust names two successor trustees. My wife is one; a business acquaintance is the other. A method for naming further successor trustees is provided. My incompetency or incapacity will be determined by my attending physician, and the successor trustees will take over on his determination. (There should be no doubt about my death.) Certain trust provisions define what the successor trustees will do with the assets during my life, and there are dispositive provisions that apply after my death. These will provide for my wife during her lifetime and may keep the property in trust during my children's lives or until they reach certain ages. Vast powers of discretion are given to the trustees. They may pay out, use, or accumulate income. They may use up the principal. They may spray the income or the principal among me, my wife and my children, equally or unequally. For tax reasons, my wife or children cannot exercise any of this discretion. But her cotrustee will undoubtedly listen to their requests. I have insisted on giving my wife (and children, when they become the beneficiaries) the power to remove the nonfamily trustee and to replace him with another who has had professional experience in serving as a trustee. This club will ensure that he pays attention, is responsive, and tries to do a good job. (Caution: The totally unrestricted right to remove a trustee by a beneficiary other than me may cause tax problems. But you can walk close to that line and get away with it.) After my death and my wife's death, when my children reach age 25 (let's say) they will receive the trust assets then remaining.

What have I accomplished? A great deal. I have not lost control. I have simplified my affairs by putting all my eggs in one basket. I have not encountered any fees (other than for the drafting of the trust) while I am the trustee. If I become disabled, the trust continues without delay as the successor trustees take over. There will be no delays while property is transferred or while someone runs to the probate court to get appointed as my conservator or guardian. There will be no additional legal costs. There will not be any question about the authority of those people handling my affairs. When I die, the same advantages will hold. Plus, the property in the trust will not go through the probate court. This will mean privacy (in that the assets in the trust do not become part of the public record) and may mean substantial cost savings (because many lawyers do not include the assets in such a trust as part of the base on which they levy their fees). I have provided for the use of the assets during my wife's life, if they are needed, but I have kept them out of her estate for estate tax purposes. I have left control in the family's hands by including the removal power. I have provided for discretionary use of the assets for my children until they reach 25, after which they are turned over to them entirely. And I have allowed sufficient discretionary powers so the income and principal can be used where it's determined to be needed by the nonfamily trustee (at least on paper) throughout.

What haven't I accomplished? I have not saved any income or estate taxes during my life because I have retained the right to revoke the trust, thereby—for tax purposes as well as for practical purposes—retaining total control over it. Oh, if it were only the other way.

What's the bad news? I've incurred a legal fee for drafting the documents.

As you can see, the dispositive provisions appear mostly in the trust rather than in my will. They may appear in my will if I want to set up a trust for my wife and children there. But if I do, I will lose all those wonderful benefits that a living trust provides.

I'm so enthusiastic about living trusts that I've actually gone out and bought one for myself.

Other uses of trusts? Here are a few quickie samples to whet your appetite:

- The use of a revocable trust to "test" the investment ability of an investment professional, to manage your affairs while you travel, or to hold the interest in a family business —and keep that interest in the hands of your lineal descendants rather than allow it to escape to the grips of others.

• The use of a "marital" trust to save estate taxes. This may be incorporated into either a living or a testamentary trust, as will be discussed two chapters forward.

• The use of an irrevocable trust to hold a term life insurance policy that your employer provides to keep the proceeds out of your estate and thus to save estate taxes.

• The use of a trust that is irrevocable for at least ten years and a day or that terminates on the earlier death of the beneficiary (the child or parent you are supporting), to save income taxes. (This is known as a "Clifford" trust, named for the taxpayer who fought it out with the IRS and won.) In addition to income tax savings, the property remaining in the trust at its termination reverts to you.

Have I started your juices flowing? These are merely hints of what can be done by a skilled practitioner. Early on, I said you should be able to do 90 percent of the planning yourself. Here's part of the 10 percent. A major part. I've given you the basics and some hints. But the execution must come from the mind and hands of a qualified pro.

Please don't conclude that trusts are only for the rich. They are not. Due to inflation and higher salaries and more investable funds, assets are piling up in our hands. Consider the use of a trust to satisfy longer-term needs as your assets accumulate. As long as you remain the trustee, the costs will not eat up the assets. And even after your tenure, by using a family member rather than a professional trustee you can continue to contain costs.

When you look to trustees other than yourself, it is of paramount importance that the trustee have huge doses of investment and tax smarts and nearly as much business smarts. Add in trust (of the normal household garden variety) and integrity, and you'll be looking at a tough role to fill. Individuals having these qualifications are rare. Lawyers having them are rarer, although many prominent law firms maintain active trust departments. Banks and trust companies also are in this business; for some people they are the only answer.

CHAPTER THIRTY-ONE

THE (REFORMED)
KILLER INSTINCT

Do you remember the old saw about the only things certain in life being death and taxes? Well, taxes are still a problem during your lively days. But when it comes to the end of those days, death becomes the only certainty. For with the passage of the 1981 annual edition of Congress's yearly attempt to keep the taxpayers guessing, the killer effect of the Federal estate tax vanished. With the passage of that act, there swept across the landscape the fresh breeze of total relief from the estate tax's clutches for nearly every man, woman, and decedent in the land. By 1987, when the provisions of the law are fully phased in, it is estimated that approximately 97 percent of us can die comfortably without incurring any—yes, any—Federal estate tax. What a change! Now we all can recoup our incentives to accumulate assets, to build estates which will be safe from diminution by the tax, and to take risks that might result in hefty increases in our net worths. What joy!

Along with the near-elimination of taxation has come another bonus for you and me: the heavy-duty estate planning needs most of us had went poof. Because of the reduction or complete elimination of the Federal death tax, estate planning has been made easier. But, please, don't fall into a trap. As I've suggested already, competency and knowledge in a professional are still vital for reasons other than saving estate taxes, although that, too, may still be a consideration for some of us. Generally, the chop in the death tax has put the focus of estate planning back where it should always have been, to "What do I want to accomplish?" not just "How can I avoid taxes?"

To describe the manner in which the Federal estate tax works, we must start with a description of what constitutes your estate. (An anecdote, if you don't mind: Way back when I first got started in this trade, my wife and I were at a cocktail party and I got introduced to a woman as an estate planner. "Just what I need," said she. My wife got excited because I needed clients to establish my business. Before the excitement spread too far, the stranger added, "An estate.")

What comprises your estate? The Federal estate tax encompasses more property than you might guess. It includes all property standing in your own name. It includes, as you already know, some portion of the assets you hold in joint names. (The amounts included, as we discussed, may surprise you.) It includes all property over which you have retained some "strings." Strings, in my graphic terminology, mean ultimate control. For example, the right to name a beneficiary under a life insurance policy; the right to revoke a living trust you created (thus my admonition that you could not escape estate taxes on the property that is included in the trust); the right to appoint the principal held in a trust that was created by someone else if you can appoint that property to yourself; even the rights granted to you under some kinds of fringe benefit plans. In sum, much more than you might have suspected. Also, in short, a rather expansive interpretation of what you "own." The Feds' idea is to "gross up" your estate to determine its value for tax purposes.

Notice, if you will, that the assets treated as part of your gross estate for tax assessment are much broader than is the property that may be included in your estate for probate purposes. The matter of what's included in your probate estate, to repeat, is decided by the law of your home state. (I might add that in this discussion of estate taxation, I am ignoring your state's estate tax. The laws of the various states differ widely. Such taxes must be considered in your thinking and planning—another reason for going to a pro—but they generally impose a very mild whack on your boodle.)

Pause for a moment, not for the drink that refreshes, but to add up the value of what would be included in your gross estate for Federal estate taxation purposes. You should have a quick fix by looking at the life insurance inventory you did for me at the end of Chapter 27. To those figures, you might add the incidentals of not-to-be-forgotten items such as IRAs, Keoghs, "lump-sum" employee benefits, things that you have retained "control" over. Got a total?

Fine. Now, we start reducing the total. The slimming-down process knocks off the balances remaining on any loans you still owe at your demise, any outstanding bills at that moment, the costs of handling your estate and any charitable gifts you may choose to leave. If you're married, you may also avail yourself of using the marital deduction. The marital deduction is an allowance for the generosity you bestow on your surviving spouse. Property you leave outright to him or her (by way of survivorship under joint ownership, as a named beneficiary under a life insurance policy or a work-related benefit, under your will, or under a trust) or property you leave under his or her control in a trust will qualify for the write-off. The choice of whether to leave it outright or in trust is another question you and your estate planner must answer. Under current law, it is possible to leave everything to a surviving spouse and pay no tax on your estate. Whether you should leave everything or less than everything is a question we will touch on in the next chapter.

After deducting all of those allowances, the calculations lead us to something dubbed the taxable estate. It is on this amount that a "tentative" tax is calculated. The figuring is done according to a tax table that resembles the one we used in working over your income tax. As with income taxes, the tax is graduated—the higher the taxable estate, the higher the tax rate. I will set out the tax table below when I give you a couple of examples of the estate tax's application.

From this tentative tax there must be a further reduction. This reduction is the exemption that is provided for the estate of each and every one of us who dies, whether we're married or single. Like the tax rates themselves, this amount is being phased in over the years. This year you can leave a taxable estate of $325,000 and incur no estate tax. Next year, the exemption will be $400,000. Then $500,000 in 1986, and $600,000 in 1987 and successive years.

I thought I heard a big sigh of relief. Your net estate is less than those amounts? Good. That proves my opening point. But don't skip the rest of this chapter. To your surprise, you may find that your assets will grow over the years (or that your debts will fall), and you may come within those ranges. Also, be cautious. You may have a taxable estate of less than $600,000, but over $325,000, and you must get safely from this year to 1987.

A monkey wrench gets tossed into our discussion. For the drafters of the tax code, nothing can be simple. Instead of taking the straightforward way of exempting the amounts of assets I just listed for you, they had to write the law in terms of "unified credits." The following may sound like doubletalk, but the difficulty is not mine. I'm merely reflecting the code writers.

The unified credit is a credit against the tax. Instead of subtracting the actual dollar value of the exemption from the gross estate value, you subtract from the estate's tax the tax stated in a dollar amount that would have been the amount of the tax at your estate's tax bracket rather than the deduction of the equivalent dollar amount of the exempted property. Got it?

Let's try it another way. If the tax were calculated on your taxable estate, the amount of the tax on $325,000 worth of property is what is allowed as a reduction in your estate's tax rather than lopping off that $325,000 amount of property from your taxable estate before figuring the tax. I'll try to make this clearer in my examples below. Suffice it to say here that instead of speaking in terms of exempted property, the reduction works in terms of a "unified credit" amount which is the tax that would have been imposed on the dollar equivalent of the exemption. For this year the unified credit is $96,300. For 1985 it is $121,800. For 1986 it is $155,800. And for 1987 and later years it is $192,800. Remember, those are offsets to the tentative tax; they are the same as exempting property from your taxable estate of $325,000 this year, going up to $600,000 in 1987 and later years.

Why is this foolishness called the unified credit? We must go off on a tangent for a few paragraphs. The tax table I'm about to present to you applies to both property transfers you make during your life and those you make at your death. The concept is that you can give the appropriate dollar-valued exempted property away either during your days or at your finale. It matters not to the code's application which you do. But you can only (with a few exceptions coming up) give away that amount of assets. In total. The amount of the credit you have not used up during your lifetime through the giving of gifts to individuals can be used to reduce your estate tax. To the extent you have used up any part or all of that unified credit amount, it will not be available to save estate taxes. The unified credit is subtracted from the tentative tax. This is done instead of letting you subtract the actual dollar value of the exemption from the gross estate value. The amount of the unified credit is equal to the tax that would be due on the exempted property, figured at the tax rate for your taxable estate. Confusing? Try it another way: In the current year, when $325,000 worth of property is exempted, it is the tax in your bracket on $325,000 that is allowed as a credit to reduce the estate tax. You subtract the credit from the tentative tax. You do not get to lop off $325,000 worth of property from your estate before figuring the tax. (I'll try to make this clearer in the examples below.)

Many lifetime gifts are permitted which have no effect on the use of the unified credit. It is possible for you to give away assets having a current value of up to $10,000 each year to as many persons as you choose. You can start by giving me $10,000—in cash or in assets of the same value. My editor would probably also appreciate such a gift. And, beyond the two of us, if you would like, you can give up to the same amount to as many other individuals as you desire. There will be no tax consequences to such gifts. The amount given will not reduce your income tax because the recipients are not charities. The gift will not be taxed to the recipients (but any future income earned on it will). However, the gifts will reduce your gross estate by the amount given, for those assets are no longer part of your estate. This gift campaign may go on year after year, whittling down your estate for as many years as you can stand it before becoming a pauper. But any gift amount in excess of $10,000 in any year to any one individual will chew up part of that unified credit amount whenever your estate tax is figured.

Well, not quite literally any gift. There are certain other exemptions that apply when you make gifts. You can give anyone any amount to cover the cost of education or medical expenses. And you can give your spouse as much as your love tells you to without incurring the gift tax. Any of these gifts may be unlimited.

It used to be better to give than to bequeath because the gift tax rates were lower until 1981. Through the "unified" approach, this is no longer true. Also, if I must remind you, any asset, once given away, is gone. Don't count on the recipient being equally as generous as you are. And you may not like the image of going back on your knees to solicit help that may or may not be forthcoming. Excluding property from the gift or estate tax by giving assets to others is conceptually an irrefutably worthwhile objective. But it has other implications. Go about it gingerly.

With the reduction in your estate's tentative tax by the unified credit, we come to the final blow—the actual estate tax to be paid. The amount I will shortly show in my examples has no allowance for any state estate tax due. The Feds allow your estate a credit against their tax for a specific amount of state death taxes paid. The amount may be more than, less than, or the same as the actual amount of those taxes, for the credit allowed is defined by the Federal code, not by the wondrous workings of your state tax wallahs.

Herewith the estate (and gift) tax table applicable to people who are so unfortunate as to die during 1984. There are different tables for ensuing years.

1984 ESTATE TAX TABLE

If the taxable estate is over the first number but not over the second number	The tax is	Plus this percent of the excess over the first number
0–$10,000	0	18%
$10,000–$20,000	$1,800	20%
$20,000–$40,000	$3,800	22%
$40,000–$60,000	$8,200	24%
$60,000–$80,000	$13,000	26%
$80,000–$100,000	$18,200	28%
$100,000–$150,000	$23,800	30%
$150,000–$250,000	$38,800	32%
$250,000–$500,000	$70,800	34%
$500,000–$750,000	$155,800	37%
$750,000–$1,000,000	$248,300	39%
$1,000,000–$1,250,000	$345,800	41%
$1,250,000–$1,500,000	$448,300	43%
$1,500,000–$2,000,000	$555,800	45%
$2,000,000–$2,500,000	$780,800	49%
$2,500,000–$3,000,000	$1,025,800	53%
$3,000,000 and up	$1,280,800	55%

The table may look bad in its grayness and enormity, but it won't appear nearly as preposterous in its applications. On to the applications.

I'm going to make you a semi-millionaire. You may scoff, but that rung is not as far off as you might have suspected before reading this chapter. By the time you add together all the property I have defined as being part of your gross estate, you take a long leg up on that sum. And what with your earning power, investment prowess, and the aid of inflation, you'll see how readily you will reach or surpass that lofty sum. I will treat you first as

SAMPLE ESTATE TAX—SINGLE

Gross estate	$500,000
minus	
Debts and expenses	
(We'll assume these	
equal 4% of your estate)	20,000
Adjusted gross estate	
(Or taxable estate in	
this case. If you leave	
anything to charity, it	
would be deducted here	
and lead to your taxable	
estate)	$480,000
Tentative tax (Determined	
by running down the	
first column of the table	
and then calculating	
across the line just as we	
did with the income tax	
table)	$149,000
Unified credit (For 1984.	
Goes up in steps to	
$192,800 in 1987, so	
watch the intervening	
years)	$96,300
Estate tax	$52,700

being single. (The same category applies if you're a widow or widower or divorced.) And then I'll deal with you as part of a deadly duet. I would hope, for purposes of saving space and repetition, that even if you're married you'll follow me through the solitary state.

As with the income tax, there is the matter of a tax bracket. This estate is in the 34 percent estate tax bracket, because that's where the range including the $480,000 taxable estate falls, as you can see from the percentage figure in the third column of the 1984 Estate Tax Table. As you can also see, the total tax due is not 34 percent of the gross estate but approximately 10 percent of it. The use of knowing your estate tax bracket is similar to the use of knowing your income tax bracket—it can help you estimate any additional tax or tax saving if you added or deleted another taxable dollar.

For the married decedent, we can start with the same figures we developed above down to the adjusted gross estate line and then subtract the marital deduction from it. I will assume, for this chapter anyhow, that love conquers all and that in a fit of generosity the dying spouse leaves the entire adjusted gross estate to the surviving spouse. The calculations would look like this:

SAMPLE ESTATE TAX—MARRIED

Adjusted gross estate	$480,000
Marital deduction (The amount left to, or for the benefit and under the control of, the surviving spouse)	$480,000
Taxable estate	0
Tentative tax	0
Unified credit (Every estate gets one)	$96,300
Estate tax	0

Marriage, in its wondrous fashion, together with the benevolent spouse's remembrance of the surviving spouse, results in the total elimination of all Federal estate taxes on his or her death, while the poor (not so poor, really) single person gets stuck. But this story does not have a totally happy ending. When the surviving spouse passes on, his or her estate will be fully subject to tax (less any charitable bequests and the unified credit). For simplicity, I will assume the surviving spouse dies in 1984, leaving the same amount of inheritance and having skipped the opportunity of remarrying. His or her estate tax would look like this:

SAMPLE ESTATE TAX—WIDOW/WIDOWER

Gross estate	$480,000
Debts and expenses (4%)	$19,200
Adjusted gross estate	$460,800
Tentative tax	$142,472
Unified credit	$96,300
Estate tax	$46,172

Without defensive measures, the total tax on the married family unit after the death of the second spouse is only modestly less than the tax on the single person. ($46,172 vs. $52,700). But the total of the debts and expenses on the two estates would more than make up for the difference: those who handle the estates do nearly as well as the tax collector. And note carefully that in the two-spouse situation it is the second estate that gets zonked.

We will survey some fundamental tax-saving techniques in the next chapter.

CHAPTER THIRTY-TWO

EASING THE PAIN

I've promised you that I'd come up with some suggestions as to how you can save estate taxes. I'm going to do better than that and give you more than you bargained for. I'll show you come tax-saving techniques, and I'll also give you a clue on saving other costs.

First, the tax savings.

All but one of these devices are available to singles and married alike.

If your estate would include more than $325,000 of assets, my first idea is that you should live longer. In coming years the unified credit will exempt assets of up to $600,000 and the maximum tax rate will fall to a level of 50 percent. This idea of living longer is, of course, presented tongue in cheek. I'm sure that if you could control that kind of planning, you'd be more than happy to make those arrangements.

If you're married and have an estate of $325,000 or less, you can feel free to leave it entirely to your charming spouse. Again, as years go by, that threshold rises and my position remains the same.

Also, if you want to have your property escape estate taxes forever, all that need be done is to make sure you're married when you pop off, leave everything you've got to your surviving spouse, your surviving spouse remarries and repeats the inheritance pattern by leaving all to his or her surviving spouse, who then follows the same routine, and so on. There might come into being a problem of generation gaps, but the use of a perpetual marital deduction will lick the Treasury. In perpetuity.

So you'd like me to stop teasing and give you some meat-and-potato ideas? Try these.

Making Gifts During Your Lifetime to Reduce the Size of Your Estate

In the preceding chapter I warned you against such an approach. My warning still stands. However, here I'm out to demonstrate how you can give wisely if you desire, and how to give so that you won't be giving away anything of current substance.

You can give wisely by staying within the limits of the $10,000 annual exemption. The clearest way to do that is to give cash or assets which do not exceed that sum. (Sage advice.) But what I have in mind is a situation where you have an asset you'd like to get out of your estate and that asset is worth considerably more than the ten-grand limit. Let's say you have a two-family house you hold as an investment and that you want to give it to your child. You could consider deeding the property to your child, taking back a mortgage and note which call for repayment on some terms, and then, every year, forgiving $10,000 on that obligation. Every year you live will exclude another $10,000 from your estate while the appreciation in the value of the house goes to your child. This arrangement could also provide you with some interest income from the note and provide your child with some income tax deductions. Now, if you "sold" the house to your child instead of merely giving it to him or her, there might be further advantages. He or she could use the purchase price as a basis for depreciating the property, and you could defer the incursion of some of your capital gain (and thus your tax) until the year you receive the partial payments. These ideas are not limited to deals with your child or deals involving only real estate. The ideas are presented to you to start your imaginative juices flowing.

You may be considered to be giving wisely if you give property that has appreciated. If you have some stock that you bought years ago and it has grown in value from $1,000 (your cost) to $8,000, you may feel this stock is the possible subject of a gift. It is, if the recipient is a charity. (More on this below.) It may not be, if the recipient is an individual. If you were to sell the stock, you would face the payment of the capital gains tax. Such a tax might be higher for you than for the recipient because you may be in a higher income tax bracket. But if you gave the stock, you would be giving an asset worth $8,000 that cost you only $1,000. Some people would consider this to be a cheap way of giving because it cost you much less. I would argue against making such a gift where the asset has appreciated substantially in value. My reasoning is that if you retain the ownership of the asset, when you die, the asset will take on a stepped-up cost basis. When your heirs go to sell the stock, their gain or loss will be figured from the $8,000 figure (assuming that was its value in your final estate valuation). The gain from the $1,000 to the $8,000 will never be taxed. Granted, we must compare the income tax rates applicable to the sale and resulting gain with your estate tax bracket to see which will be less costly. But my standard approach to the situation in which you have a substantially appreciated asset is to hold on to it and to let the estate tax step-up do its wonderful thing. If the asset has appreciated some but it is not expected to grow much further, feel free to give it away. When the asset has lost value, hold on to it if you can use the loss to offset gains or to reduce your taxable income. And who can't?

One type of asset you can give away without hurting yourself currently is a life insurance policy. A policy (assuming it has no cash value) has only a contingent value: it will have value when you die, but currently, without cash value, it has no value. (If it does have a cash value, borrow it out before making the gift I'm about to propose.) You can make a gift of the policy to the person you have named as beneficiary. By transferring ownership, the policy proceeds will not be part of your estate and will, on your death, be paid to the beneficiary whom you wished to receive the proceeds. These proceeds will be undiminished by any estate tax since they were not part of your estate. (Watch it, for by giving the policy, as I've said, you've truly given it away—the new owner then has total control over it. This is no more than a repeat of my routine warning that making a gift is making a gift.) How's that for form without substance?

Making Gifts to Charities Will Save Estate Taxes

A gift of that $1,000–$8,000 appreciated stock we were discussing will save some income taxes if made during your lifetime. You heard earlier that you will get a deduction for the value of the stock at the time of the gift and will pay no capital gains tax on the amount of the appreciation. What I have in mind here is the use of a charitable gift to save estate taxes. As with the stock, you can make a lifetime gift and get that property out of your estate. Such a gift may include all or a portion of your assets. Further, you can bequeath your entire estate or a portion of it to a charity and have that amount excluded from your estate. There are a few "giving" plans that almost every charity can explain to you. Generally, they combine some form of charitable gift with income and estate tax savings and the provision of income to you during your life, and possibly to your heirs on your death. The tax savings are heavy, but the property is the charity's, and the giving decision is final. In a few situations, however, such gifts make sense.

Using Trusts May Reduce the Amount of Assets That Are Part of Your Gross Estate

I'll give you two tastes of this fruitful idea.

The first has to do with term life insurance policies. In a way, the idea of "gifting" them which I described earlier will do the same thing I'm going to mention here—it will get the proceeds out of your estate. But what I have in mind here relates to those policies that come with your job. Say you have a large amount of assets already and, through your work, you have a $100,000 term policy. By establishing an irrevocable trust and assigning that policy to it, you can exclude the policy proceeds from your estate, have the trust provide exactly what you would want to have done with the proceeds anyway, and really give away nothing. Although I have singled out a work-related term life insurance policy as the asset in my suggestion, the concept of using an irrevocable trust has other uses. It's just that they may be trickier because there may be gift tax problems. Once again, the decision to use an irrevocable trust is a grave decision.

My second idea is the use of trusts to keep assets out of other people's estates. Establishing a trust as described in the preceding paragraph should do that if you provide that the property in the trust will be used by a trustee for someone's benefit during his or her lifetime rather than being distributed (turned over) to the beneficiary. That will keep the property out of the beneficiary's estate. Of course, the trustee should be given discretion to use the property for that person's needs, as we've already discussed. And these ideas can be used in trusts for spouses, children, siblings, friends, anyone. It may also be possible to achieve the same tax savings in one or more generations.

To demonstrate what this approach could save for a married couple, let me use the same numbers I used in the last chapter and, instead of assuming that the dying spouse (whom I will call "he") left everything to the surviving spouse ("she"), I'll assume that he left half of his adjusted gross estate to his spouse either outright or in trust for her benefit. (If it's left in trust, she must receive the income from the trust property during her lifetime and must have the right to decide where the trust estate goes on her death, even if she does not choose to exercise the right. She may also have other rights which the creator of the trust, in his discretion, can bestow on her under the document.) As you will see, the significant gain occurs at the death of the second spouse.

Here's what his estate tax calculation would look like:

HUSBAND'S ESTATE TAX

Gross estate	$500,000
Debts and expenses (4%)	$20,000
Adjusted gross estate	$480,000
Marital deduction	$240,000
Taxable estate	$240,000
Tentative tax	$67,600
Unified credit	$96,300
Estate tax	0

As was true with the case where he left everything to her, there is no tax on his estate. By using a marital deduction of half the adjusted gross estate and the unified credit, all taxes have been eliminated on his estate once again. Actually, the amount of the marital deduction could have been reduced to the point where his estate had as much as $325,000 worth of assets in it left subject to tax and it would have still not incurred any tax. So, the inter-working of the marital deduction and the exempted property under the unified credit can reduce or, as in this case, totally eliminate the tax on his estate. The marital deduction may include all of his assets or something less than all. How much is left after the marital deduction depends on what sums we are talking about and the full use of the unified credit on both estates, as we shall now see.

Assuming she dies in 1984 without remarrying and without any changes in the value of the assets, here's what the tax calculation would look like on her estate:

WIDOW'S ESTATE TAX

Gross estate (The amount left to her by the marital deduction taken in his estate)	$240,000
Debts and expenses (4%)	$9,600
Adjusted gross estate (or taxable estate)	$230,400
Tentative tax	$64,528
Unified credit	$96,300
Estate tax	0

What have we done? Most importantly, if you look back to the previous chapter and note the amount of estate tax on the second spouse's estate, you'll see we have obliterated a tax of $46,172. A neat little saving. How did we do that? By having the marital deduction in the first estate cover less than all of the assets in that estate, by keeping the remaining assets in the first estate to a level that was less than the amount represented by the unified credit, by keeping the non-marital portion of the first estate in a trust and thus out of the second spouse's estate, and by generally "balancing" between the two estates the total assets in such a way as to maximize the effects of the marital deduction and the unified credit in both estates. This idea of balancing each spouse's estate is another valuable estate planning tool. (These other ideas of using trusts and taking full advantage of the unified credit available to every estate can save taxes for more than married couples.)

We have done one other thing in this last example. We have saved nearly $10,000 in administrative expenses in the second estate. We have done this by excluding a major portion of the assets from the second estate through the use of a trust for the non-marital portion of the first estate. In essence, we have saved 4 percent of the value of those assets. I have been using this 4 percent figure as an estimate of what the administrative expenses would run. They might be higher or lower, but this is more than a reasonable estimate.

My bonus for you in this chapter is that a large part of these administrative expenses may be saved if you buy my recommendation of using a living trust. By doing so, there will be some saving in legal fees. Even if we assume that only half the normal fees would be saved with having all the assets held in a living trust, the savings would be tremendous. Take the case of the single person in the last chapter. His or her estate swallowed administrative costs of $20,000. If all the assets were held under a living trust and the legal fees were cut only in half, there would be a saving of $10,000. In the case of the married couple, the costs were $20,000 on the first estate and $19,200 on the second estate, or a total of $39,200 on both estates. If the assets were held under a living trust, if that trust provided for a marital deduction trust on the death of the first spouse and a non-marital deduction trust to be held along with that trust for the lifetime of the surviving spouse, and if the legal fees were assumed to be halved by excluding these assets from the basis for figuring the legal fees, the savings would run to nearly $20,000. More for the heirs, less for the lawyers. By keeping the assets in the trusts and thus out of the probate proceedings there may be additional savings in court costs. (True, there would be trustee fees. But I would argue that with the proper selection of trustees and with the necessity for on-going assistance in management of the assets anyway—as opposed to the one-shot death services—there will still be big savings.)

I hope these suggestions give you a flavor of what choices you have available to you in this area. If I've tickled your fancy and you'd like to pry further into these matters of estate planning, you can refer to a thick paperback entitled *Estate Planning Guide*, written by Sidney Kess and Bertil Westlin and published by Commerce Clearing House.

CHAPTER THIRTY-THREE

A BAND-AID
FOR AN EMERGENCY

Finally, in this list of defensive maneuvers (and just before you collapse in a state of exhaustion), we come to a consideration of what is truly your first line of defense when an emergency strikes: some available cash.

When you need it, you need it. The available cash must be there. You've got to get your hands on it. It is this available cash that keeps your financial ship afloat. Without having it, you're figuratively adrift at sea, subject to being buffeted about by even the smallest of rolling waves, and at high risk of being swamped by a rough sea. The real function of having such funds available is to give you staying power. Having ready funds buys you time when a surprise or a shortfall hits. The time buys you some room to think, as well as the opportunity to make a rational decision as to where to turn next if additional funds are required. Along with those advantages, the time may save you from having to sell an asset at the wrong moment or from having to settle for a disastrous price. These are enormous plus-factors.

How much of an emergency fund do you need? In nearly every situation, I feel that an emergency fund equal to one-fourth of your ongoing annual expenses should provide adequate protection. For situations where your income is irregular or highly volatile or where your comfort level requires more, add a little more to my minimum. The minimum amount should be derived from the budget figures you developed for me when we were first getting acquainted. Take the total of your annual expenses from that budget, deduct from those total expenses all of your income-related taxes and your allocation for your programmed savings, and divide the remaining number by four. Shooting for that amount as an emergency reserve should take care of you.

Clearly, you want these funds to be liquid. You also want them to be safe so that you don't want to have to worry about them, or for that matter even pay any attention to them. You want them to be there when you need them, and to be there with absolute certainty. You want them to be conveniently accessible. You may want to have other services made available by the holder of those funds. (Such as providing a safety-deposit box or offering loan funds.) You want as high a return as you can get from an account which offers these characteristics, but you are not seeking to maximize the return as you would if you were looking at these funds as investible dollars.

In brief, I have described a "savings" type of account.

What alternatives do you have available to you that would meet these requirements?

Essentially, there are two alternatives: (1) your friendly, neighborhood banking institution, or (2) a money-market mutual fund.

With the advent of their own money-market accounts, banks offer a viable alternative to mutual funds. These accounts are slightly over a year old and permit the bank to pay a competitive interest rate on your deposit rather than the traditional, restricted rate of 5 or 5½ percent. You must maintain a minimum balance of $2,500, and there may be some minimal restrictions on the minimum amount you can withdraw each time and on how many withdrawals or deposits you can make monthly. But the characteristics I have described for you are there (assuming the bank is covered by Federal Deposit Insurance Corporation—FDIC—insurance). And the return you receive is right up there with current rates.

In some states (such as mine, Massachusetts), there may be state income tax advantages to the choice of this kind of bank account in comparison with a money-market mutual fund account.

I will include in my definition of banks those institutions known as credit unions. These are a rapidly growing and highly competitive kind of financial institution. They are formed by their members for their own benefit and have increasingly expanding authorities. Because they are operated for the benefit of the members and are expected to be "non-profit," there may be some advantages in using one if one is available to you. Generally, credit unions pay higher rates of return on deposits and charge lower rates of interest on their loans than do competing financial institutions. But you must make absolutely certain that the credit union you use is backed by the National Credit Union Administration (a Federal agency similar to the FDIC).

Money-market mutual funds are only slightly more than a decade old. They were founded by the mutual fund industry to provide a vehicle for pooling my few dollars with your few dollars and investing in vehicles that you and I could not afford individually because we had so few dollars and the minimum prices of admission were so high. These funds buy investments known as money-market instruments. Money-market instruments are interest-paying obligations of various kinds sold by issuers who need short-term money and are willing to pay a good rate of return. All money-market investments mature within one year from their issuance date, and the vast majority of them mature in a much shorter time, which might be as short as a day. These investments are usually sold in minimum amounts of $100,000, although a few may come down to a $10,000 minimum. That is certainly not low enough for most of us to sprinkle our dollars around in a few issues. These instruments also entail varying degrees of risk so that protection is engendered only by prudent diversification.

When the mutual fund industry applied the pooling idea to money-market investing, the sales of such funds shot into the stratosphere and stayed there until banks got authority to establish money-market accounts of their own a little over a year ago. The pendulum now is swinging in favor of the banks because they offer the safety of the FDIC insurance, which none of the mutual funds have. To counter this, some funds are purchasing insurance from private companies.

Safety can be obtained through the back door in using a money-market mutual fund by watching what its portfolio of investments includes. A fund which invests only in securities issued or guaranteed by the U.S. Treasury Department is certainly safe even though it has no insurance. To the extent that the fund's portfolio includes other investments, there is a declining degree of safety in most cases. But your return presumably will increase.

How much risk are you willing to assume for how much of a difference in return?

Safety apart, these funds offer you the same benefits a bank money-market account does.

The choice is yours. My point is that the possession of such an emergency fund is an absolute necessity.

PART FOUR

OFFENSE

CHAPTER THIRTY-FOUR

ON TO FUN,
FORTUNE AND SATISFACTION

The past, as some venerable logician once put it, is prologue. What we've done up to this point is to get your financial affairs in order and guarantee their solidity. This is a jumping-off point. From here, we look at what you can do in the future, what objectives you'd like to reach, and what investment vehicles will best enable you to reach those goals. Also, I'd like to have the privilege of calling your attention to some off-the-wall-sounding approaches to advancing not only your money matters but your psyche as well.

What you will encounter in the next few chapters are the comments of a stodgy, crusty, timeworn investment professional who has been hardened on the anvil of experience. In some places my expressions may sound too harsh. In some I may sound too inflexible and stubborn. In some I may sound narrow-minded, blinded or unreceptive to opposing thoughts. If you read me in any of those fashions you may be correct, but keep in mind that I am trying to do several things for you: (1) Share the lessons of years of experience. (2) Have you benefit from my mistakes so your education won't be as costly in time or dollars as mine has been. (3) Stick to the simple approach because it still works. (4) Inform you of one man's approach to an investment program that produces results without risking the bundle. There are, without argument, other approaches which also work. There may be as many approaches to investing as there are investors. You should develop your own after having profited from the advice of other people (including me). The one that is best for you is the one that fits you, and no one (again including me) can pontificate for you.

I must warn you that this is an "approach" book. It is written to give you the framework within which to operate, the words to know so you won't be aghast in disorientation when someone starts unloading the jargon, and the reassurance to handle nearly all of your affairs yourself. This part of the book will not make you an investment professional or offer you a discussion in encyclopedic depth on every subject. If you want to delve more deeply into any subject, you can dabble with a few pennies to learn by doing. You can go to your nearest adult education provider to learn by hearing. Or you can select from a voluminous library of learned treatises on every facet of the investment jungle. If you do the latter, I would like to humbly request that you consider my two earlier books *Buying a Condominium* and *The Small Investor's Guide to Large Profits in the Stock Market,* both brought to you by the same wonderful publisher who put this tome into your hands. Both books are, I hope, easy to read and apply and are presented in a step-by-step cookbook style.

The objective of every investment program should be to build capital. The sole purpose of that building is to achieve some degree of financial freedom—either total, if you're successful enough, or partial, if your successes are modest. Forget what the money will be used for. You can use it for anything once you've gotten it. Our job is to get it, and to get it in a way that will be comforting, steady and, yes, even fun. This accumulation of wealth may give you personal satisfaction in and of itself, or you may get some of that pleasure from the activities you are pursuing or some of the specific assets themselves. Forget not that the rewards can be emotional and psychological as well as monetary.

CHAPTER THIRTY-FIVE

IF YOU DON'T KNOW WHAT YOU WANT, YOU'LL NEVER GET IT

Throughout this work, I have on occasion referred to some financial goals and made some recommendations on how you might achieve them. You've heard about goals such as getting the most from your budget, saving taxes, reducing insurance costs, avoiding probate and probate expenses, and a few others. There are, if you can stand to hear a secret, other financial goals that you might covet. May I suggest you might want to maximize your investment return? Or provide an education fund for your children? Or create a worry-free retirement for yourself? Or fight inflation?

Most of these goals center on investment decisions, as I've remarked more than once. Choosing the investment that will produce the highest return is the only significant factor in these decisions. Of course, in nearly every one of these selections tax saving is part of the maximization of the investment return. I will comment in the following chapters about my feelings as to which investment makes the most sense, both before and after tax. Some goals, like building a college or retirement fund, may also require the choice of a method for reaching the goals in addition to the selection of an appropriate type of investment. Again, tax considerations play a part. More on these matters in a moment.

First, I'd like to talk generally about setting and reaching goals.

Take a trip with me. I live in Cambridge, Massachusetts, the center of the universe, in some peoples' minds. I take a ride to Cape Cod nearly every weekend. The Cape, as we Bostonians call it, is about eighty miles away. I have several choices of transportation to get there. I can drive, take a bus, fly, or if I have the time, walk. Assuming I stick to the ground, my route could follow one of several roads. I may not always take the shortest route. I may want to take a side trip, or stop at a restaurant or visit Plymouth to kiss the Rock. On my journey, I mentally lop off the mileage markers and tick off the exits from the expressway.

I take you with me on this pilgrimage not to provide you with a tourist's view of the scene, but to use the trip as a model for a goal-setting exercise. My destination is the Cape. I have several choices as to the route I will follow to get there and the method of transportation I will use to get there. I may make zigs and zags along the route, but I get a sense of approaching my destination each time I pass a mileage marker or an exit. In addition, at any exit I can decide to take a diversion and head out in another direction.

The same flexibility exists in setting financial goals. To take an example, storing up enough beans to buy a home may seem like an insurmountable task. You may need thousands of dollars more before you get there. But, if you set your sights at shorter distances and make a game of reaching those shorter objectives, piling up the funds for the purchase will not seem as insurmountable. At each level, you will be saving toward the objective and gaining a sense of accomplishment at the same time. Always, you will be working in the general direction. But you will also preserve some flexibility and choice along the way. Different investments can be used to accumulate the necessary money. As your money grows, you may still decide that some other objective is now more desirable for you. You have the luxury of using those funds for that purpose instead, if you choose. Only when you plop down that pile of greenbacks at the home purchase have you finally reached your long-term goal, and even then those dollars are not gone forever but may serve further financial goals. (Such as buying a bugger home or a second home, or paying for a college education, or serving as a source for retirement funds.)

This is the way I like to think of establishing financial goals. Set a long-term objective way off in the future or requiring a very substantial pile of money that you don't currently possess. Work toward that goal constantly, choosing various methods to pursue it but veering in different directions in the short hops as opportunities arise. Keep your sights on the goal, but mark off shorter steps that will build toward the longer one and give you the satisfaction of licking them. Make the first step simple and easy to reach, and your confidence and determination will get a boost. Flexibility is paramount. As I believe you will recall my mentioning, it is the accumulation of those dollars that is important; how you use them may change over time.

There are two goals that tend to get many individuals hung up: education and retirement planning. They are, no doubt about it, essential goals to consider. Unless you are immediately upon them, there is much that can be done. I'll try to describe each of them separately.

We'll start with the education planning issue, for it may present a sharper focus. Assume you determine how much you will need by taking a year's anticipated expenses adjusted for inflation, multiplying that amount times the number of years of education to be undertaken, and then multiplying that by the number of children you are planning to pay for. That number will give you the target to shoot for. How much do you have set aside now to start with? What's the difference between the amount you need and the amount you have on hand? Divide the difference by the number of years you've got to amass the fund, and you'll see what you must shoot for each year. (Divide that figure further by twelve, if you'd like to look at it on a monthly basis.) Where is that sum going to come from? Out of your budget, possibly. More likely, out of an investment return. (In some cases you may want to raise the lump sum out of borrowing or take it out through the total depletion of an asset.) Where can you get that investment return? How can you maximize that return to save taxes or to accumulate faster?

Here's where you might consider the use of a custodian account or a trust, if you have the necessary assets and you can afford to set them aside into such an account. Either of these, as we've seen, will save income taxes and may save estate taxes. If you can't use one of these accounts, you probably will want to seek capital gains because of the tax break they provide.

Unlike education planning, where there is something resembling a firm target to shoot at, retirement planning may offer a mushy target. One way to fix a target is to use your current budget as a guide and guess at an annual inflation rate before you compound that rate for the number of years you have to reach retirement. This mechanism is spongy because it has too many assumptions built into it. Who knows what the inflation rate will be? Who knows what your budget will look like then? Who knows where and how you'll want to live? Who knows what the tax rates will be? Who knows which assets you might use to produce income or what your investment return on them might be? In spite of these uncertainties, this rough approximation will be better than nothing if only because it gives you some number to work with.

My conclusion is that you'll need as much in retirement as you can get. Let's fire on all fours to get what you can. Generally, this means that your retirement funds will come from several sources. They will come from some governmental program (such as Social Security, if you're subject to it). They will come from some employer-provided programs (if you're an employee and if your employer has such plans). They'll come from some program you've contributed to yourself (such as your contributions to a thrift plan or a 403b plan). They'll come from some plan you've initiated yourself (like a Keogh Plan or an IRA). And, finally, they'll come from the assets you've been able to accumulate as part of your regular investment program. This last source may be the most significant.

All of these, if I must be the messenger bearing the bad news, will be essential. None can be counted on as being adequate by itself.

Where you have any choice as to the type of investment to be used under any of the tax-favored umbrellas, my strong preference is for an investment which offers the advantages of safety, stability in value, regular and rapid compounding, high and consistent return, and little or no attention. Add to these the desire to hold the overhead expenses to a minimum. My whole idea is to provide for a stable fund that simply snowballs at as rapid a rate as possible and that will be there when you need it without causing you concern or requiring time to manage while it accumulates. If you buy these characteristics, they point to the use of a short-term, interest-bearing investment—money-market mutual funds, money-market bank accounts or short-term U.S. Treasury investments.

I would argue that investing in stocks or other investments that may provide capital gains is not as attractive as these types of accounts. For one reason, there are the joint concerns of safety of principal and volatility of price. For another, there is a huge benefit in having profits taxed at capital gains rates, but if you were to take these gains under a tax-favored umbrella you would not get the full advantage of those tax breaks.

It is for this last reason that I would invest for capital gains purposes in your "regular" investment program rather than in one that resides under a tax-favored umbrella.

As you can see, certain types of accounts aimed at specific purposes may require investment programs specially designed to hit their targets. In the next chapter, I will describe the structuring of an investment program that is not bound by these specificities but is one that fits your general needs.

Goals, then, must be defined and investments must be selected to fit the achievement of those goals. This selection combines consideration of both the specific characteristics and benefits an investment can offer in terms of its return with understanding and maximization of its tax aspects.

CHAPTER THIRTY-SIX

THE LAYERED LOOK

In designing an investment program, there are three separate layers of holdings to consider. The allocation of your assets among the three layers and the composition of each layer are very much custom-tailored determinations reflective of your individual needs.

There are many factors to be considered in customizing an investment program for you. These factors include your age, your family situation, your current and projected income levels, your current and anticipated asset levels, your present and expected tax situation, potential inheritances or the receipt of substantial gifts, the possible requirement that you provide significant support to a relative or someone else, your knowledge and experience, your determination, your risk-taking nature, and your likes, dislikes, hopes and fears—to name several of the considerations. You can see from this list that the blending of assets in the composition of your investment program is not something that can be imposed upon you by dictate or standard formula. Yet many people try to do exactly that. No, my belief is that the investment program you live under should be developed exclusively for, and even by, you so that it satisfies your needs and permits you to enjoy peace of mind.

The factor that has the most effect in determining the composition of your investment program is your need to raise current income from your investments. By golly, if you need current income, you need current income; there is no way around it.

Naturally, then, the first layer to consider in establishing an investment program is what I call the income layer. How much income do you need annually in addition to your income received from other sources?

Take a simple example. Suppose, according to your budget, you need an annual income of $15,000 (to pick a non-intimidating number). From your work you pull in $14,000. You are "short" $1,000. Among your assets, you have $20,000 of investible funds. You know from reading the papers and listening to the nightly news you can get 9½ percent from a "safe" investment such as a bank money-market account, a money-market mutual fund, or a Treasury obligation. How much must you invest to make up that shortfall of $1,000? Divide the $1,000 by 9½ percent (divide by 0.095, not 9.5), and you get $10,526.32. This is the sum you must invest at 9½ percent to get your $1,000. That is, assuming you need your $1,000 as a before-tax income. If you need the $1,000 in after-tax income, you multiply the 9½ percent by your tax bracket, since your tax bracket rate will chew up some of the income if it is taxable income. Assume you're in the 30 percent tax bracket. Multiply 9½ percent by 30 percent (0.3) and you come out with 2.85 percent. Taxes will eat up 2.85 percent of your income. Subtract that number from the 9½ percent to get what will be left for you after tax. The correct answer, in the event your math may be rusty, is 6.65 percent. Divide the $1,000 of after-tax income by this 6.65 percent (0.0665) and you will find you must invest $15,037.59 at 9½ percent to have your $1,000 left after tax if you are in the 30 percent tax bracket. So I've given you the calculation two ways: One assuming you were looking for that grand before tax and one assuming you wanted it net after tax.

This exercise is premised on the idea that you must raise the $1,000 from your investments. Not everyone is in a posiiton that forces them to raise any money from their investments on a current-income basis. (Lucky dogs.) For them, the income layer of an investment program may not be a necessity for the production of income, although it may serve another purpose.

This income layer provides a few further advantages. Usually, the investments held in it are relatively safe. Usually, they are relatively liquid. And usually, they are relatively stable in price. I inserted "usually" because whether or not those attributes are present depends on your specific selection of investments. I would recommend that you make sure at least part of your holdings in this segment of your investment program possess these features. My reason for this suggestion is that these assets should buy you additional time in raising funds if you need additional money over and above your emergency funds. Your emergency funds will buy you up to three months. This layer is where you would look next if you need additional money. Thus, even if you don't need to raise income from some portion of your investment program, having some sum in the income layer would be advantageous. How much? Whatever you're comfortable with. Another three months' expenses? Maybe, but only if you're super-cautious.

The second layer of your investment program should focus on growth. You should hold assets in this layer which have the potential to appreciate in value. I would say that everyone, regardless of age, sex, or status needs some growth. Why? Because of inflation. These assets will represent a base for deriving income in the future, and the larger the base the more income it will generate. The question to be answered, as it was in the income layer, is how much should be invested in this layer. I would say that for those in the younger age bracket (20s to 40s) the amount should be a large proportion of your assets—perhaps 50–60 percent. For those in later years, the proportions should be lower but never, as I've said, absent. There are a couple of reasons for this age discrimination. One is that the younger you are, the more time you have for these assets to work for you, and they will take time to appreciate. Growth in value—substantial growth—does not happen over ten minutes. Also, being younger, you are theoretically more capable of dealing with volatility in values. And, to state the obvious, you are less dependent on these investments for income because of your larger earning power, and you have time remaining ahead of you to recoup any losses.

At the top of the investment program pyramid is the aggressive layer. It is dubbed aggressive because you are stepping into more speculative areas of investing with the hope that you will make a bigger killing. This layer does not belong in everyone's investment program. It has no place for those very close to, or already in, retirement. It has no place for those who abhor "risk" or broad-sweeping price volatility. For others, it has a place, but only for a tiny portion of your assets. Maybe I should say no more than 10 percent of your assets, but this amount should be viewed as a guideline rather than an absolute limitation. I offer it only in order to show relative proportions.

With this pyramid in view, I must discuss the various types of investments available for your selection and make an attempt to review what types might fit into each layer.

As we have three layers in our investment program, so, too, is the number three appropriate when it comes to discussing investment types, for there are basically only three types of investments available to you. (1) There are debt types, under which you make a loan to someone who agrees to repay you the amount of the loan plus interest for the rental of your money, and to pay both of these according to terms embodied in the loan instrument. (2) There are equity types of investments, under which you become the owner of an asset or part of an asset and celebrate all the rewards and suffer all the woes of being an owner. (3) There are hybrid types, which combine elements from both the debt and equity types into a mixed bag of benefits and detriments that usually results in your riding a horse with two heads. (Or two tails.)

Which of these types of investments fit into our three-layered investment program? Any or all can fit into any or all of the layers. Let me demonstrate by listing investments of each type under each of the program layers. We will examine them individually in the next several chapters.

The Income Layer

- Debt investments
  Bank accounts of every nature
  Holdings in money-market mutual funds
  Obligations of the United States or its agencies
  Obligations of a state or any of its subdivisions
  Obligations of a corporation
  Loans to another individual

- Equity investments
  Common stock
  Preferred stock
  Investment real estate
  Mineral rights
  Annuities

- Hybrid investments
  Convertible preferred stock
  Convertible corporate bonds

The Growth Layer

- Debt investments
  Bonds of the Federal or a state government or of a corporation which are selling at a discount from their face value

- Equity investments
  Common stock
  Home ownership
  Other real estate
  Tangible property
  A business

- Hybrid investments
  Convertible preferred stock
  Convertible corporate bonds

The Aggressive Layer

- Debt investments
  Bonds of a state government or of a corporation selling at a discount from their face values

- Equity investments
  Common stock
  Options
  Commodity interests
  Futures
  Tangible property
  Investment real estate

- Hybrid investments
  Convertible preferred stock
  Convertible corporate bonds

Some of these labels may require definition. I will handle that in succeeding chapters.

Some investments fit into more than one layer. This is because, although the type of investment is identical, the characteristics of the specific investment chosen may differ. Again, I will say more on this as we go along.

Each of these investments can be invested in directly, or indirectly through the use of a pool. (Some assets are most commonly bought directly. They include bank accounts, annuities, homes, tangible property, and a business. Of course it is possible, but perhaps not attractive, to make such investments as part of a pool.) We have already discussed the use of money-market mutual funds. This is one kind of pooled investment. But, as I say, any of the other investments also can be made by investing in a pool which, in turn, invests in them. Through pooling you can participate indirectly in investments that you could not purchase directly on your own because you don't have enough money to do so. I will discuss these pools further in Chapter 43.

For now, let's consider whether you should invest directly on your own or whether you should join a pool.

The decision is based first on the amount of money you have available to invest in the specific layer and the specific investment within the layer. If you don't have enough to invest in either the layer or the investment, you are forced into a pool. If you have enough money to invest directly, but not enough to invest in a diversified sampling of holdings, I would suggest that once again you are ticketed for a pool.

Other than the limitation imposed on you by the size of your wallet, you may feel uncomfortable making decisions or handling the mechanics of the transaction on your own. You may not feel you have the knowledge or the confidence; you may not have the time or the aptitude to bother; you may not have the inclination to deal with the numbers or the analysis; or you might just be lazy. No problem. These are some of the reasons the pools exist.

But, where possible, I strongly prefer a do-it-yourself approach over a pooled approach. My reasons will become clear as we go forward.

CHAPTER THIRTY-SEVEN

RENT FOR YOUR MONEY

The list of potential borrowers of your money is endless. It runs the gamut from a buddy at work all the way up (down?) to Federal Big Brother himself. The best way for me to have you consider to whom you might want to lend your money is to present each potential borrower to you and then to look at the kinds of questions you might want to have answered about those borrowers before forking your funds over.

Let's start with your bank. When you make a deposit in your bank, you are in fact lending your money to the bank and becoming a creditor of the bank. The bank is indebted to you, if you can imagine such a turnabout. The bank permits you to choose among several types of loans you can make to it. You can make a demand deposit (to your way of thinking, a checking account—which in its negotiable order of withdrawal, or NOW, incarnation at banking institutions pays interest), make a savings type of account deposit (which now, in its money-market trappings, pays a competitive rate of interest), make a term deposit (meaning it cannot be withdrawn before a specified maturity date), or purchase a certificate of deposit (another name for some types of term deposits). The minimum amount you need to take advantage of these choices varies between $10 and $10,000.

Next on your list of prospective borrowers I'll put the Federal government. It may do its borrowing through the Treasury Department or it may do it through the auspices of one of its agenices. If done by the Treasury, the borrowing may be called a treasury bill, note, or bond. Bills are obligations of the Treasury which mature in either 91, 182 or 364 days from their issuance date. The two shorter maturities are sold weekly. The year bill is sold once every four weeks. These instruments require a minimum purchase of $10,000 in face amount (with additional purchases of $5,000 above that) and have two special twists. First, they are sold at a discount from their face amount so that, if you buy one with, say, a $10,000 face value, you will pay less than that. The amount you will pay depends on the quoted interest rate. Because you pay less than the face amount, your effective yield is higher than the quoted yield. (Approximately half a percentage point more, in ballpark numbers.) Second, they pay their interest at maturity by paying their full face value.

Treasury notes and bonds are similar to one another except that they differ as to their maturity dates. Notes, when they are sold, pay you back in anywhere between one year and ten years, depending on the maturity date the Treasury puts on the issue. Bonds have a maturity date of more than ten years from the date of their sale. Each pays interest every six months and is usually sold at its face amount when it is sold at its issue date. According to the terms of the sale the Treasury sets on the specific issue, the minimum may be $1,000, $5,000 or $10,000.

The obligations of the various Federal agencies are called notes, bonds or debentures (a form of bond), depending on their maturities. These maturities may run anywhere from six months to forty years from the date of their initial sale. Minimum face amounts available for purchase my be $1,000, $5,000 or $25,000.

Any of these government securities may be bought after their initial offering in the open market. One consequence of this is that you can pick your maturity date by selecting a security that will mature on the date you are seeking to have your money available.

We turn next to the so-called municipal bond market. This name encompasses all the obligations which are issued by a state or one of its subdivisions or are guaranteed by one of those governmental bodies. There are several categories of "municipals." The usual breakdown is into general obligation instruments (those carrying the backing of the full taxing power of the municipality), revenue bonds (those dependent on the revenue-generating capability of the debtor), and special purpose issues (those such as industrial development bonds under which a facility is built for, and leased to, a corporation to attract its presence, or dormitory bonds that are used to finance the construction of housing which is then leased to a college). These obligations are called notes if they mature in a year or less from the issue date, or bonds if they run longer. Typically, they are sold in $5,000 minimums. The short-maturity obligations pay interest at the end; the longer-term obligations pay interest every six months.

Corporation obligations, known as notes, bonds or debentures, depending on their maturity dates and on the assets that may stand behind them, are usually sold in minimum face amounts of $1,000. Interest on these loans is paid every six months.

Finally, I bring you back to your buddy. He (or she) may cajole you into lending him or her anywhere from a sawbuck up to a million. The terms you work out are what you can negotiate.

Now that you've met this cast of characters, what factors run through your mind in trying to decide where to lend your money? Obviously, I would not ask that question if I weren't prepared with an answer. Before I give you mine, take a minute and think it through for yourself, and then we can compare notes. No pun intended.)

Ready?

Well, we've already considered the minimum amount of threshold. Do you have enough bucks to pay the price of admission? If so, do you have enough to obtain a few of the goodies to achieve some diversification? (If you deem that to be necessary, and I do except where you're using a bank.)

Now we move on to the more interesting concerns.

What about safety? Which are the safest, and which are the more risky? Generally, the risks are in the order I introduced them to you with one minor repositioning. Those issued by (or others that may be guaranteed by) the U.S. Treasury are, in the trade, considered the safest. Next come the Federal agencies and the banks (assuming they have government insurance on their accounts). Then follow the municipalities, with gradations according to the types of securities under investigation. And then the corporations, again in varying gradations. And, at the bottom of the ladder, that lonely old buddy of yours.

Some of these investments, such as the municipals and the corporates, are evaluated by rating services that grade the quality of the obligation in terms of your risk as a lender. These ratings are done by independent firms (for example, Standard & Poor or Moody) and are on an alphabetical ranking (AAA, AA, A, B, etc.). These ratings may change from time to time during the life of the obligation and should not be relied on for your decision simply because the rating is currently superb.

What abour reward? If these investments represent differing degrees of risk, shouldn't they provide differing degrees of return? Well, generally yes, but not absolutely yes. In theory, the higher the risk, the higher the interest. But there are some quirks. Six-month bank certificates of deposit, for instance, may pay the same quoted interest rate as treasury bills of the same maturity, but your actual yield will be higher on the T-bills. That's because the effective rate is higher since the bills are sold at a discount. And the interest on the bills is free of state income tax, which may not be the situation with the bank interest. (Also, you may be able to sell the bills without penalty if you need your money before maturity.) I take the position that if risk is present, a higher interest rate does not compensate you for taking on additional risk. It will, if you get repaid. But it won't if you don't. Someone can quote you a rate of 30 percent interest, but if they can't pay it, what good was the promise?

Which brings us face to face with the interest rate. This is, as you can see, another feature to consider. Not only the promised rate as we were considering it, but also when it is paid, how it is compounded (if it is), how the dates of the interest payments fit in with your needs, and whether the interest is subject to all income taxes or is free of either Federal tax or state tax or both. (On this last score, don't jump at an issue simply because it's tax-free. It's your net after-tax return which counts. I'll show you how to determine your net after-tax yield at the end of this chapter. This may sound like kindergarten stuff, but I've seen too many adults swoon over it and then live to regret it.)

And what is the likelihood you'll get paid? Both interest and the repayment of your principal? Are you able to fit the date of repayment into your scheduled need? Do the interest payment dates come when you want them to, when you need the income?

What kind of collateral can you recover if your borrower goes belly-up? Is it collectible? What is its likely value?

What if you must cash in or sell your investment ahead of its maturity date? Will there be a penalty? Can you, indeed, sell it? Is there a market for your investment, and how precise are the prices in that market? Consider, for a moment, municipal obligations and corporate obligations. Although they both can be purchased in smaller denominations, they are usually traded in "round lots" of $100,000 of face value. If you buy (or, God forbid, sell) a smaller face amount, you'll very likely get creamed on the price. And, unlike treasury or Federal agency issues, there may be limited price visibility. You may not be able to pick up your *Wall Street Journal* and fix your eyes on a price set by an actual trade. You may be at the mercy of your bank or broker as to what's a "fair" price. (Fair to whom?) And, worse still, for some of these investments and certainly for your loan to a buddy, there may be no market at all. No one may want to buy from you, at any price.

What are the expenses related to the acquisition or disposition of the investment? If you use a bank account, there should be none. If you buy your treasury obligations directly from the Federal Reserve Bank in your neighborhood, there should be none. If you buy those securities or any of the others from your bank or broker, there will be some, both on the purchase and the maturity (or sale) of the securities. On transactions involving smaller amounts of dollars, these charges may wipe out any possible benefits from higher interest rates.

Generally, the farther off the maturity date the higher the interest rate the investment will promise to pay. Many investors "reach" for yield; they stretch the maturity dates of their investments to get these higher returns. Or, to put it in what are considered to be more favorable terms, they want to "lock in" a high-appearing interest rate. There are considerable risks attendant upon doing this.

Time for another one of my small slices of life to demonstrate a few principles.

Assume that my good friend Woeful bought a $1,000 corporate bond five years ago and paid the full price of $1,000 for it. The bond will mature in the far-off future. Assume that at the time he bought it, it had a triple-A rating and that it carries a 9 percent coupon rate (its stated annual interest rate). Woeful thought he was doing the brightest thing he could do. He had a good quality bond. It paid a high return, the highest he could get at the time. The bond was issued by a first-class, premier corporation so he felt he could sell it if he needed to. And here we are, a mere five years from the time when Woeful bought his bonanza. Let's assume that bonds with the same maturity date being sold today by companies of the same quality are paying 12 percent interest.

Woeful is saddened. He could be getting 12 percent each year instead of the 9 percent he's stuck with. He can't sell his bond for what he paid for it. In effect, he's locked in, just like the interest rate he locked in.

Along comes my one and only other friend, Shrewdy. Shrewdy has $1,000 to invest. He's considering buying either a new bond or Woeful's bond. If he buys a new bond, he can get 12 percent on his money because that's what the current going rate for such bonds is. But he can also get 12 percent by buying Woeful's bond. How? By paying him less. How much would he pay Woeful if he wanted to buy Woeful's bond and get a 12 percent return? $750. How did I get that? By dividing $90 (the annual interest on Woeful's bond, figured from the face amount of $1,000 multiplied by the coupon rate of 9 percent) by 12 percent (the rate currently available on comparable bonds). That is, $90 annual interest is 12 percent of $750. Check the answer: multiply 12 percent times $750, and you will get $90. Shrewdy can buy a new bond with a 12 percent coupon or buy Woeful's bond with a 9 percent coupon for $750 and still get a 12 percent current yield.

Let's look at the decision from Shrewdy's side first. Which should he buy? It depends on several factors. If he needs the 12 percent return on his total $1,000 to generate $120 for current income requirements, he will buy a new bond because Woeful's will only pay him $90 a year. If he's in a high tax bracket, under certain circumstances he may prefer to get some of his return in the form of a capital gain (the bond is scheduled to pay $1,000 when it matures, and he's paying $750 for it) instead of ordinary income tax on the interest. If his crystal ball tells him that interest rates are going to drop before the bond matures, he may get a higher profit from the new 12 percent bond. Or, if he continues to conclude that interest rates may drop, he may instead decide to buy Woeful's bond because of his fear that, if they do drop, the company issuing the new bond may call its bond, pay off the loan and issue a new bond at a lower interest rate to save money. The higher-coupon bond is more likely to be called in such a case than is the lower-coupon one because rates must drop a great deal farther to reach below the 9 percent level. (This "call" provision exists in nearly all corporate bonds, most municipals, and only a few Federals. It gives the issuer the right to call the loan at some point, usually five years from its issue date, at a price only slightly higher than the face amount of the bond.) If the bond is called,

Shrewdy will have to reinvest his funds at the then-prevailing interest rate which, by definition, will be lower, or the company would not be calling its bonds. Not an easy decision for Shrewdy.

For poor old Woeful, there is no decision. He has made it when he bought the bond. (And it will be the same for Shrewdy when he makes his decision. For his bond, whichever it may be, will do the same unto him as did Woeful's unto him.) Woeful, having bought his long-term bond, can only lose. If interest rates go up, he will hate himself because he would like to be getting a higher interest rate than he is locked into. He will be unhappy unloading his bond because he will not want to suffer that 25 percent loss of capital we have calculated. If the interest rate levels go down, he will be in clover until his bond is called. When it is, he will be forced into the marketplace at a time when he can only get a lower rate. So he, as a bond buyer, is taking on the risk of changes in interest rates.

He is also taking on the risk of inflation. At maturity, he will get—at most—the face amount of the bond. The money will be worth something less than it is worth today. How much less depends on the inflation rate between now and then.

He is also taking on the credit risk of the issuer of the bond. At the time he bought it, it was rated triple-A. That rating may have changed or may yet change prior to maturity. The company may not continue to be of the same creditworthiness it was when he bought the bond. And, as I've pointed out, there is the risk of having his bond called if interest rates drop. These last two risks can be eliminated by buying only Federal obligations. There is (in theory) no credit risk with Uncle Sam, and almost none of his debts are callable. So the coupon rate is protected for the life of the bond.

All of these risks are present in any debt investment. Of course, I've painted them as bleak as I could. Shrewdy would, in fact, pay slightly more than the $750 I've been using. The reason is that there are two elements involved in his return—one is the stream (trickle?) of interest payments until maturity, and the other is his profit (or loss) which will be realized on the maturity of the bond. Both of these ingredients are used to figure the so-called "yield to maturity" which should be the basis for comparison in determining whether one bond or another is the more attractive. The actual price Shrewdy would pay would be determined by the coupon rate and the remaining years until the bond's maturity. Since, in my example, we don't know that date, we can't figure the exact price. But when you're considering buying debt securities, inquire of your banker or broker or check this number in the daily price quotations in the paper. If Shrewdy pays more than $750, Woeful's loss will be less than 25 percent but, I can tell you from experience, will still be high percentagewise.

I can hear you cry out that there may be an advantage in here. Turn Woeful's misery to Shrewdy's advantage. Build capital (forget the tax business) by buying bonds selling at a discount. Fine. If the time till maturity is fairly short (no more than two or three years) and the creditworthiness of the issuer is beyond reproach, by buying at a discount you will get to keep the spread between the price you pay and the face amount. It is this point I had in mind when I put Federal, municipal and corporate bonds on the list of debt investments in the growth layer of your investment program. I also put the municipals and corporates down as possible investments for the aggressive layer. Same point; only a matter of degree. If the credit risks are greater or the maturity dates later, the risks—and, hopefully, the returns—may be greater. But remember, you can't have it both ways. If you make money on the maturity because of the spread between what you pay and the face amount, it means you settled for less current income than you could have otherwise obtained, so your gain may be partially illusory.

Suppose you say that buying a debt security doesn't require you to hold it until maturity and that you can trade in (buy and sell) debt securities to take advantage of changes in interest rate levels. The result of making this statement is the same as are the consequences of buying a debt investment in the first place. You are, in essence, predicting what interest rate levels will be. No one, not even you, can do that. Not consistently. You may hit it lucky once or twice. I believe that interest rate levels are totally unpredictable. As the next step to this conclusion, I concentrate on using short-term debt investments (those having a maturity of one year or less). I try to break the money I have for the income layer into equal dollar amounts spread out at three-month intervals and reinvest that amount when it matures. I will buy two, three or four pieces, depending on the total dollars, and have one of those pieces mature every three months. When it does, if I continue to use this type of investment, I will reinvest it to fit the regular three-month pattern. This will not only greatly reduce the harmful effects of using debt investments I've been relating. It will also allow you to get a second look each time you have something maturing. You can ride with changing interest rates much more closely or you can choose to invest in some other investment, new or with better potential. Generally, I use treasury obligations to do this. But in making my decision, I go through the following calculations on the alternative choices which are then available to me. Assuming that all alternatives have the same maturity date, do the following for each of them and pick the best one:

EVALUATING INVESTMENT RETURN

Amount to be invested   _____
Type of investment   _____
Coupon or stated rate   _____
Projected annual income (multiply the
    dollars you are going to invest by
    the coupon or stated rate)   _____
Subtract any Federal income tax
    (multiply the projected annual
    income by your tax bracket)   _____
Subtract any state income tax   _____
This is your projected net annual
    income   _____
Divide the net annual income by the
    total dollars you are investing and
    multiply by 100 to get the net
    percentage return   _____

It is this net after-tax yield that is the one you should concentrate on regardless of whether or not one of the alternatives you are considering has "tax free" tattooed on its bold banner. Even where the tax-free alternative shows a slightly better return, I'd pass over it because of the other issues I've discussed. Largely, I feel that the government gives you the luxury of tax-free interest but wipes you out by destroying your principal through inflation. Unless you have gobs of money and spread out your maturities to counteract interest cycles in a fashion similar to what I described in using short-term Treasuries, I'd say ignore the municipals.

CHAPTER THIRTY-EIGHT

OWNING A COMPANY

Buying shares of stock makes you a partial owner of a company. As an owner, what can you expect for your investment?

There may be two types of rewards. The first may be sharing in some of the profits earned by the business. Your share of the profits comes to you in the form of cash dividends, which are the amounts of the annual profits the company's board of directors decides to distribute. As you may guess from this description, the payment of dividends is not a guaranteed thing. There must be earnings, and then the board of directors must decide whether or not to distribute some portion of those earnings and, if it decides to distribute them, what portion. The second kind of reward you may receive as an owner is the appreciation in the market value (selling price) of the stock. Again, this is far from being assured. But, the theory goes, if the company continues to prosper, the market price of its shares will advance. Depending on what your needs are, you may be investing for one or the other of these rewards or, like me, you may be looking for a combination of both. This combination is referred to as a "total return," meaning your rewards are made up of some segment of both a current dividend and an increase in the stock's market price.

We saw the same concept when we were considering interest-paying investment. We were talking of both the current interest rate the investment paid and the maturing of the investment at full face value after you purchased it at a discount. With interest-paying investments, you could be nearly certain that your "total return" expectations would come to fruition if you selected carefully. Your interest payments were fixed. You could easily determine what your profit would be on maturity by subtracting your cost from the investment's face value. Here, in investing in stocks, your total return is not determinable until after the fact. Once you sell your shares, you will know what your total return has been. Only then will you accurately measure what dividends you have received and what market appreciation (or depreciation) your shares have enjoyed during the period in which you held them. Going in, everything is based on expectation.

With a stock purchase you are buying the future of a business. Whether you invest $1,000 or $100 million, you must think of your investment in those terms. The best way to attempt to gauge the future of a business is by looking at its past and making assessments of its potential. Already, I'm sure you realize, we're taking a great leap of faith. One part of that faith is that the history is accurately recorded. Another is that we can read it correctly. Another is that it is appropriate to project from that foundation. Another is that our assessment of its potential is correct. And still another is that the marketplace will recognize the potential and actual business results and award a fair market value to the price of the shares. That's what we're counting on.

In truth, the company's business prospects and results may march to one tune and the price of its stock to another. These movements do not have to be in tandem. Many times, the market cycle may reflect anticipation rather than reality. And, many times, the market may have other influences awash in it. What is the level of interest rates? (Yes, this has an effect.) Is there a recession going on? What about inflation? Moon phases? Skirt lengths? Super Bowl winners?

How can you tell what's going to be? You can't. And as an owner you take on not only the rewards I've mentioned but also the risks of ownership. These include the business risks, the market risks, and the risks prevalent in the psychology of the time. No one can scientifically define this bundle of risks. It is my thesis that you don't have to. All you have to do is to measure some probabilities—some odds—and get them working for you rather than against you. I will demonstrate what I mean shortly.

First, let's speak of the two types of stock you can purchase and study the differences between the two. For good measure, I'll throw in a variation on one of the types.

The first type I'd like to discuss is preferred stock. This is a type of ownership interest which, by its name, has some preferences. What can they be? They are of two kinds: preference when it comes to dividends, and preference when it comes to dissolution rights. The dividend preference says that if the board of directors of the company decides to declare a dividend on any class of stock, it must first pay the dividend on the preferred stock before it can pay any dividend on the common stock (the other type of stock ownership). The second preference says that in the event of the dissolution of the company, the assets remaining after all creditors are paid are distributed first to the preferred stock owners and then, if any remain, to the common stockholders. These are the preferential rights.

Preferred stock carries a fixed dividend rate. I mean that the dividend is set at the time the stock is first sold to those of us who choose to buy it, and the dividend does not change during the entire time the preferred stock remains outstanding. (Of course, there is no guarantee that a dividend might not be skipped if there are no earnings or if the board does not declare one.)

What have you bought if you've bought preferred stock? Not much. A fixed dividend. (At the very start of your investment this gives away one of the real rewards of being an owner: the chance to get higher dividends as the earnings of the business increase.) Because the dividend is fixed, the market price of the shares follows very closely the swinging cycles of interest rate levels. As those rates increase, your share price will go down, just as we saw with my two friends Woeful and Shrewdy. But unlike the bond those boys were playing with, these preferred shares have no maturity date. The company never has to repurchase them unless it wants to. Thus, you may be on an eternal roller coaster and never get to the end of the ride. Lastly, I would suggest that if you're investing in a business, you're doing so not for its worth on dissolution but for its worth as a going concern. It's got to be worth more as a viable, breathing entity than as a carcass to be nibbled on by vultures. Hope, anticipation, and expectations offer excitement and profit. Carving up a cold turkey is clinical.

Why buy these foolish things? Who said you should? They are appropriate only for other corporate investors. A corporation can receive dividends from another corporation, and 85 percent of those dividends are free of Federal income tax. A neat bonus for a corporation, but not for kind, old you. Many of "yous" are attracted to these shares by what may appear to be their high current yields. Resist the temptation.

To counter objections such as those I just raised and to appeal to more potential investors, some companies issue a variation on the bread-and-butter type of preferred stock. Out they come with a convertible preferred stock. It is similar in all ways to the regular preferred stock I have been describing, but it has another feature: it can be converted into shares of common stock at a predetermined rate. The idea is to put some fun into your life and to make the opportunity more enticing. With convertible preferreds the stimulation is that you can make a bundle because of the seemingly favorable conversion rate. You get your dividend. You also get your action by tracking the price of the common stock with the price of your preferred and by drooling over the killing you're going to make on the conversion possibility. Well, maybe you will, maybe you won't. Some investors have been successful at this. Not me. I feel your preferreds are neither fish nor turkeys. The company will put a lower dividend rate on them than would otherwise be the case because of the convertible "kicker." And the lure of the kicker is usually disproportionate to what the realities may, in practice, be.

I think you've got to decide—are you playing the game for the income or for the appreciation? (As I said, I like to play it for both. I'll squeeze another comment into these parentheses. Throughout this discussion of convertible preferred stock, you can substitute convertible bonds and reach the same results. The only difference is that bonds pay interest instead of dividends, and that their interest is a fixed requirement rather than being dependent on the existence of earnings and the mood of the board. Also, being bonds, they carry a repayment date. So?)

This leads me to a discussion of common stock. This kind of ownership is, for me, far and away the most appealing. As is implicit in some of my earlier comments, you get a shot at a dividend which can increase (or decrease) as the company's earnings increase, and you get another shot at that price-per-share increase in the marketplace. Both of those shots can be highly rewarding, and both can offer protection from inflation.

But not all common stock investments are created equal. Companies, like humans, go through different stages of life. There is birth, infancy, youth, adolescence, maturity, middle age, old age and death. Depending on what your objectives are in investing, you may choose to make investments in companies which are in one or another of these stages. Speaking in generalities, those companies which come at the earlier stages of this spectrum tend to offer a greater potential for appreciation in share prices but little or no current dividends. Again speaking generally, those companies which are in the center spread of this spectrum tend to offer a modest degree of price appreciation potential and a greater dividend yield. Still speaking generally, those companies which are at the older end of the spectrum tend to offer more price and dividend stability. And generally, once more, those companies which are at death's door offer as much, or greater, risk as those at birth. Only speculatively can they be said to offer anything in the way of either price appreciation potential or dividend rewards.

In any investment program that includes common stocks, I like to concentrate on the adolescent stage primarily when I am looking for investments for my growth layer. Naturally, you can see from my lifelike display, some companies may fit into either the income or the aggressive layer as well. It is the characteristics of the particular company that decide where it fits into your program.

Those characteristics may be determined by looking at the financial report of the company and by looking at its other characteristics. I will take you through a quick financial analysis in a minute. But first, consider the other, non-financial characteristics. You can compose a list broader than mine. The list should include all of the fundamental considerations you can think of. Use your own common sense. I'll get you started. What's the industry? Its markets? Are they growing? Is the product or service useful? How? Is it costly? What of competition? Labor skills and costs? Who are the managers? Would I be proud to be an owner of this business? You can see the range of questions I'd consider.

Now to the numbers.

Essentially, there are four groups of numerical measurements I look at, those measuring:

- Growth
- Profitability

- Creditworthiness

- Value

I figure that if those factors are working for you, it's awfully hard to go wrong.

The growth rate of a specific aspect of a company you are considering is determined by taking the number for one period and dividing it by the number for the same aspect from an earlier period. I'll bring all of these calculations down to earth by using some demonstration numbers from one of my favorite companies, a company I'll call Glop Corporation. (Not its real name, to be sure. The name I am using as a disguise came from one of its annual reports. In it, the president of the company said that many people asked what his company did, and he described it as making "glop." Actually, the company manufactures chemical specialty products—specially designed formulations to satisfy customer needs.) Let's say we are considering Glop's growth rate in its earnings per share. That's the amount of profit it makes in a given year for each share of common stock that is owned. Let's say that in Year I Glop earned 98 cents per share and in Year 5 it earned $2.11 per share. Not a bad increase.

There are several ways of measuring at what rate Glop's earnings growth occurred. One way is to say that from Year 1 to Year 5, its earnings per share increased by 115 percent. (Divide $2.11 by $0.98, multiply by 100, and subtract the 100 percent you started with as a basis for measurement.) Another way is to say that over the four years (that is the actual span because Year 1 was completed before you had a base to start figuring from), the earnings per share increased at an average annual rate of nearly 29 percent (115 percent divided by 4). And still another way is to say that Glop showed a compound growth rate in its earnings per share of more than 21 percent per year. (I got this number from a table of compound growth rates, but perhaps your calculator, unlike mine, has a key to figure this.) Whichever one you use, you can see that Glop's earnings per share from Year 1 to Year 5 have done very well. The point is that the growth of a company, and of its specific financial features that you choose to measure, is essential to the success of your investment. Rapid growth may mean high appreciation. It may also mean high increases in dividends. (Over the same five years, Glop's dividend went from 19 cents to 34 cents per share.) The slower the growth rate, the more plodding the stock price and the dividend growth.

Profitability is also crucial to the success of your investment. A company can sell a ton of glop, but if those sales are not profitable it will be digging itself into a deeper mire. Profitability usually is measured in two ways: (1) How many pennies out of every sales dollar the company gets to keep as profit. (2) How much profit it makes on what its shareholders have invested in the business. Looking at Glop's figures for Year 5, it had sales of $76.1 million and total net earnings of $7.8 million. Its profit margin, the number of pennies on every dollars of sales it keeps as profit, was slightly greater than 10 percent (7.8 divided by 76.1, times 100). Its return on stockholders' equity, or the profit it made on what its shareholders had invested in the business, was 22 percent. (Divide the $7.8 million net earnings by $34.9 million, times 100. This amount is shown on the company's balance sheet as "shareholders' equity.") Both of these measurements are extremely attractive. If the business is this profitable, shouldn't you want to be an owner?

Next, we look at its creditworthiness—its financial soundness, its strength to withstand the throes of business warfare and cycles. One measure of a company's creditworthiness is its ability to pay off the bills which are due in the next year out of the assets it has on hand or that will come into its hands during that year. For Glop, this calculation would show that it had nearly three times as many "current assets" as it had "current liabilities." Another way to look at a company's creditworthiness is to look at how much of the total permanent capital invested in the business is from long-term borrowing, compared to the amount from stockholder investments. For Glop Corp. in Year 5, the number is zero. It had not borrowed a dime. (Wouldn't you like to be in that situation?) These tests show a company's staying power, its ability to last. These financial underpinnings tell you how peaceably you can sleep at night as an investor. Put another way, they tell you what kind of business risks you are running. I don't see any with Glop.

On to measurements of value. As with the others, there are several, but I'll concentrate on two. (1) The price/earnings multiple. This tells you how many years of earning power is reflected in the current price per share. To determine what it is, divide the current price per share by the current earnings per share. In Glop's case, the current price is $12.875, its current earnings per share are $2.11, and its price/earnings ratio is 6.1, meaning you would be paying about six years of current earnings for a company that has been growing at the compounded annual rate of 21 percent over the past four-year period. In general, the higher the price/earnings multiple, the riskier the investment. (2) The current yield. This is determined, as we did with Woeful's bond, by dividing the current income (in this case, the annual current dividend of 34 cents a share) by the current price of the investment ($12.875 a share). Glop's current yield is 2.6 percent. This is certainly lower than even a bank account pays.

Wanna buy Glop? If you need current income, the answer may be no. If you want future, high income and/or a shot at that appreciation in price, the answer may be yes.

I played a sneaky game with you. Although Glop does indeed exist and although the numbers I used were actual numbers from its experience, in fact Year 5 was five years ago. I did it to you because I wanted to solidify my case for making stock investments.

Precisely at the end of five years from the numbers I have been using, Glop's common stock was selling at $27.50 a share, and its current annual dividend was 68 cents a share. If you had bought the stock at $12.875, you would have shown a long-term gain of $14.625, or 114 percent, in five years, and your dividend would have doubled in that period (from 34 cents to 68 cents). The yield on your original invested dollars would have also doubled to 5.3 percent because of the doubling dividend. Still not a great current yield, but together these numbers could mean an annual return of about 28 percent. (The 114 percent gain divided by 5 for the number of years you would have held it gives you 22.8 percent annually plus the current 5.3 percent dividend yield.) Magnifique. Total return.

Ah, if everything were only Glop.

I use it to show you why common stock investing makes abundantly good sense (in every environment as long as you have the luxury of being able to wait it out) and to give you a flavor of what goes into the decision-making process. If you're stimulated to swallow more, try my *Small Investor's Guide to Large Profits in the Stock Market* mentioned earlier. If you're stimulated by curiosity, pull out your own stock holdings and run some of these measurements to see how well your companies are doing.

And, hey, the sooner you get your dollars working in this manner, the longer you'll have to let them work. That's all it takes: Some understanding, a consistent system; and time, wonderful time.

CHAPTER THIRTY-NINE

ODDS AND—NO ODDS

Before leaving the realm of security investments, we should pause briefly to consider some of the more aggressive ventures open to your speculative urges. Action, you want? Action, we got. The following comments are X-rated, so please use your discretion and remove anyone younger than 21 from your proximity while reading this.

Start our unexpurgated list with options. Options give you the right to buy or sell (depending on which you invest in) a block of 100 shares of common stock at a set price within a limited period of time. You can exercise this right at any time up to the date on which the option expires. For this privilege, you will pay a premium. The premium is the price of the option (not of the stock) and it is set by market conditions, which reflect many factors including, among other things, the length of time remaining before the option expires, the striking price at which the option can be exercised, the volatility of the price of the underlying shares, general expectations about the market and the company's potential, the mood of the public, and the weighted average of the normal daily consumption rate of raspberry sherbet over a twenty-three-year period in the twelfth century B.C. Taking all of these data into account, the premium on the option usually turns out to be somewhere around 5–10 percent of the value of the underlying stock's price at the time the option comes into being.

Take an example. Suppose the price of a share of Micromystique is now at $50. You can buy an option to buy 100 shares of Micromystique for a premium of $250. This option will entitle you to buy the 100 shares at any time between today and six months from now at the same price it is selling for today, namely, $50 a share. (I am simplifying numbers to some extent.) The reason for your buying the option is that you expect Micromystique shares to be selling for far more than $50 a share within six months of today. The math looks like this: If you were to buy the 100 shares, you'd have to shell out $5,000 today. You may not have that sum of dollars. If you do, you may not want to put it into one holding or you may not have enough additional dollars to be able to diversify your holdings. You may not want to put all that money at risk in Micromystique. Also, you reason, if Micromystique's share price goes up to $55, you will make $500, or 10 percent on your money. I know you. You're greedy. That's just not enough of a return to keep you happy. You want more. You consider buying the option to buy the 100 shares instead of buying the 100 shares themselves. How does this work? You lay out the $250 which gives you the right to buy the 100 shares at $50 a share within the six months. If the share price goes to $55, your $250 would enable you to buy an asset now worth $5,500. You could exercise your option, buy the stock for $5,000 and immediately resell it for $5,500, leaving you with $500. Alternatively, you could short-cut part of the shenanigans and sell your option at a price which would approximate the same number of dollars of profit. Either way, if you took the profit you'd be making $500 on an investment of $250. Whoopie! 100 percent profit. And in no more than six months' time. Can't beat that. If, sadly, the price of the underlying stock stayed at $50 or, worse still, fell below that price, you would watch your option expire without exercising it and expire having no value. Your $250 would be lost and gone forever. Sorry. One way you make 100 percent, and the other way you lose 100 percent. Or it might result in your making something in between or even a higher profit.

Let's put this option under a microscope (not a product of Micromystique) and see what you're really getting. You're getting a glimmer of hope and a load of tension and excitement and, if you're very, very lucky, a good profit. In reality, the vast proportion of options expire unexercised. The main reason is that the probabilities don't work. When you paid your premium in our Micromystique example, you were immediately "down" 5 percent. In any buy-option position, what is the likelihood that the price of the shares will move by at least the premium percentage? If they move no more than that, or if they fall, you're a loser. Now add the time constraint. Assuming they can, in fact, move up enough to get you even, how likely is it that they will move that much in such a short time? You put yourself behind on two scores—price and time—and either one of them by itself may be taking on a whole lot. True, if all goes according to your hopes, you can make a big percentage gain.

Why are options so popular if the odds are so poor? People love the action. Small moves in stock prices can translate into big moves in option prices. The swings may be wide. The volatility may be invigorating. You can never lose more than your premium. The size of that premium is relatively small. And you can "control" an asset worth many times your investment. Not to mention the huge percentage reward if it works. Brokers love to sell them. Their commission may run as high as 20 percent of the premium, and they may be able to generate as many as three commissions by making the original sale. Goody, goody. (A broker friend of mine refers to options as alligators: they eat up your money.)

Granted, I've simplified the numbers considerably to demonstrate the concept and have only looked at the option to buy some shares. You may take an option to sell. Or you may be on the "selling" side of the option. Each of these may have its particular nuances, but conceptually the description holds. I don't use options at all.

If you think the odds are against you in the options business, don't even get anywhere near the futures markets. These markets give you, for the payment of a price, the right to buy (or, in some cases, sell) some quantity of something somewhere down the road at an established dollar value. This something may be pork bellies, corn, silver, soybeans, or some other commodity. Or, taking the idea one step further and taking the commodity out of the process, you may be gambling (note the choice of words) on what the six-month treasury bill rate or the Dow-Jones Industrial Average (the most commonly quoted stock market indicator) or the pound sterling may be at that point down the road. Action, there certainly is. Volatility, there certainly is. Precision in the pricing of your investment, there certainly is. Long odds, there certainly are. Big killings, there certainly may be. And your total wipe-out is certainly very likely. Opportunities for cardiac arrest abound. There may be some legitimate economic reasons for many heavy-roller participants to play these games (such as to hedge their bets on changing price levels). But for innocent you, what else can there be except speculation? Can you take on the likes of major corporations and governments and expect to come out clad? Not in this game. And, if I must be somewhat outspoken (which, you know, is not my bent), some of the commodity stuff may be rigged. I have no hard evidence to support that statement, but there are grounds for my suspicions. And the same opinions have been forthcoming from some respected authorities.

Spin the roulette wheel. Take to Las Vegas or Atlantic City. Buy a lottery ticket. The odds might be better.

CHAPTER FORTY

A ROOF OVER YOUR HEAD

A roof over your head does more than keep your hair dry. Most important, it gives you the warm glow of being secure in your home, of being safe from a forced relocation, of having the peace of mind that tingles your nerve endings with a feeling of belonging. These psychic rewards are worth more than any financially measurable ones. They come not from being a tenant but from being a homeowner. You've got roots. Your home colors your entire being, setting your attitude for the full twenty-four hours of every day. With those moderate comments, I begin my chapter on homeownership. This investment is one for the growth layer of your investment program. (If you approach the decision looking for investment rewards, you're looking at homeownership as an aggressive investment, and you may be sorry.) As primarily a residence, and only tertiarily as having investment potential, you should not go wrong over the years.

I will now speak in bullish tones.

Owning a home is the keystone of both your investment and your tax planning. From the investment side, it gives you an asset which should hold its value or increase in value. Your home is, in fact, a valuable asset in many ways. You can use it, borrow on it, swap it, improve it, rent it, sell it, or do a few other things with it. It thus has many facets to its value. It should provide protection against inflation. As the cost of land increases and as the cost of replacement increases, so too should the value of your home. It brings your monthly carrying costs into focus, and it may keep them very close to the level at which they stand. As time passes, these carrying costs should represent a declining percentage of your income as your income rises and your costs remain relatively stable. In any event you have some control over them. You may not have as much control as you'd like, but you do have some. When you sell, you very probably will recoup those costs.

On the tax side, my litany is almost as long. At the very least, the real estate taxes and the interest on any mortgage you may have are deductible on your federal income tax return. Almost always, the amounts of these two overhead items (or, in many cases, either of them alone) are sufficient to get the total of your deductibles over the threshold of the zero bracket amount. If this occurs in your case, the other expenses you pay that were not in themselves or in total adequate to get you over that barrier now become deductible. These other expenses may include things like your state income tax, your sales tax, interest on other loans, charitable gifts, professional dues, safety-deposit box rentals, investment journals and courses, tax-form preparation fees, and similar items. By increasing the list of possible deductions, you may lower not only your taxable income but also may push it into a lower tax bracket.

Longer term, there are further tax breaks. If you sell your home at a profit, it is considered to be a capital asset. If you owned it for more than six months, any gain would be taxed as a long-term capital gain. If we stop here, you'd be paying a tax at its most favorable rate. But if you went on and purchased another principal residence at a price which is at least equal to the sale of the principal residence you're selling, no gain would be recognized for tax purposes. And you could keep pushing off the day of the recognition of that gain as long as you kept pushing up the price of the home you buy to at least the price level of the one you're selling. Forever. At age 55, there's another break. This one lets you show a profit of up to $125,000 and not pay a single cent of tax on that profit. You must have lived in the home for at least three of the five years preceding the date of its sale, and the residence must have been your principal residence to enjoy this tax-free advantage. But what a neat bonus. What a way, for instance, to build another nest egg that may have some retirement benefits; $125,000 tax-free is still more than lunch money in today's environment.

My bullish remarks apply whether your home is a single-family house, part of a two- or three-family house, a cooperative apartment, or a condominium. It must be your residence (and, in some cases, as I've indicated, your principal residence), and it must therefore be a home that you use (as opposed to an investment or business use).

What you can afford in terms of price is a function of how much you have available to make as a down payment and what you can afford to pay in monthly carrying costs. I'll give you a ridiculous example to demonstrate what I mean. Assume your gross annual income is $18,000. By a sleight of hand, this makes your gross monthly income $1,500. Assume that you have to borrow some part of the cost of the home you want to buy and that your lender follows the rules I gave you very early in this book. (For a stodgy lender, your mortgage payment plus real estate taxes and insurance on your home cannot exceed 28 percent of your gross income. For a more realistic lender, those expenses plus any payments on other obligations cannot exceed 36 percent of your gross income.) You have no other loans outstanding. You want to buy a $45,000 home. (Don't gag. Remember, it's a demo.) Try these different situations:

	Down payment (as percentage of the purchase price):			
	10%	20%	30%	40%
Purchase price	$45,000	$45,000	$45,000	$45,000
Mortgage amount	40,500	36,000	31,500	27,000
Cash down payment	$4,500	$9,000	$13,500	$18,000

A problem exists already. Do you have that kind of money to enable you to make the down payment? Many people, today, don't. The number of individuals having the amount necessary to put down on a home has declined dramatically over the past few years. Those who can make the price of admission have, generally, gotten their funds from the sale of another home, from family aid, or from hitting a bonanza of some kind. If you are among those of us who are less fortunate, where can you get the down payment money? Sell something. Anything. (I had a client who found he had the down payment on a home in his stamp collection sitting in a cardboard box under his desk.) Borrow from cash value life insurance policies. Borrow from family. See if your employer has a program you can tap. Be creative in your solution.

Mortgage-money sources may be just as varied as the sources for your down payment. Traditionally, thrift institutions (savings banks and savings and loan associations) have been the primary sources of mortgage loans. Today, the competition has heated up and there are numerous possibilities: banks, credit unions, mortgage companies, possibly even insurance companies, brokerage firms, employers, pension funds, other individuals, even the seller of the home.

Passing to the next set of limitations, the monthly carrying charges, here's what each alternative would look like:

	10% Down	20% Down	30% Down	40% Down
Mortgage payment	$397.31	$353.16	$309.02	$264.87
Real estate taxes	178.13	178.13	178.13	178.13
Total monthly payment	$575.44	$531.29	$487.15	$443.00
% of gross income	38	35	32	30

Now we have viewed the second limiting factor, the percentage of your gross income that is eaten up by your housing payments. (The percentage of gross income figures were derived from your $1,500 monthly gross income and the total monthly payment figures shown.)

For mortgage terms I have used a direct-reduction type of loan having an 11 percent interest rate and being fully repaid after 25 years. This type of loan has a constant monthly payment in total dollars, but each month more of the payment goes toward the repayment of the principal amount of the loan and less goes toward interest as the loan balance amortizes in the direction of zero with each payment. Traditionally, this type of loan has been the most common. From time to time, however, other types of loans have prevailed. These modifications of the traditional direct-reduction mortgage fade in and fade out as economic cycles push inflation rates (and thus interest rates) up and down. These modified types of mortgages are designed to achieve one purpose—to make housing affordable to more people who might not otherwise be capable of meeting the payments. Honestly, there may be another purpose. To keep the lender from getting stuck at the short end when interest rates rise.

There are standard mortgage payment tables available which give you the numbers for monthly payments under different mortgage terms. These tables are available from financial printers, in libraries, from lenders and from real estate brokerage offices. I took my example payments from such a table, but the real estate tax figure is only an estimate.

Looking at the table I gave you, if you were the prospective buyer I described, which mortgage could you, in the lender's eyes, afford to carry? If the lender is the stodgy traditionalist, none of them. This is because, under none of the alternatives would the total monthly payment come within the top-side figure of 28 percent of gross income going for housing costs. If the lender went to the more realistic 36 percent maximum figure, the buyer could qualify under any of the last three alternatives. This qualification problem is another aspect of today's housing market. Fewer than one-fourth of all American families can qualify to carry the current monthly payments necessitated by high housing prices brought on by inflation and high interest rates. What does that tell you about the potential for substantial price appreciation?

It tells me that it may be limited. If so few people can afford it, the number of people comprising the market must also be somewhat limited. If the market is limited, there may not be much demand. If there is not much demand, prices may not skyrocket. And, if inflation does not escalate to double-digit levels soon, there may be even less pressure on pushing prices up. With the absence of tremendous price appreciation and with comparatively high carrying costs, could not tenancy be a better deal right now? It could. But please reserve your final judgment until I lead you through my story.

If I were to tell you that I bought a home for $22,000 fifteen years ago that is currently worth $95,000, would you be envious? Probably. If I were to add that, at the time I bought it, I was able to obtain a 6 percent mortgage which is still taking a little better than $122 a month, wouldn't you be even more envious? Very definitely. You'd hate me. Well, go ahead, for those numbers are true. It sounds like a sweet deal. Be jealous. But let me recast the purchase in another light. Follow me through these calculations:

Purchase price	$22,000
Mortgage amount	18,000
Cash down payment	$4,000

Here are the cash outlays I've made over those fifteen years:

Cash down payment	$4,000
Mortgage payments	22,036
Real estate taxes	10,500
Utilities and heat	13,500
Insurance	4,500
Maintenance/improvements	7,100
Total cash outlay	$61,636

To the best of my recollection, those were the outlays. I've made an honest effort to come close on all of them and not to leave any out. But who knows? Over fifteen years, a lot may slip from memory. Far better to have kept records.

Consider now my tax savings over that period. Again, my records are incomplete. But I'll try to ballpark it and to do that in a generous way—perhaps overstating my tax bracket for all those years to show a higher tax saving than I might have enjoyed. Total income tax deductions over the fifteen years:

Mortgage interest	$12,036
Real estate taxes	10,500
Total tax deductions	22,536
Estimated tax savings	$10,141

The mortgage interest figure came by subtracting the difference between the original amount of the loan ($18,000) and its current remaining balance ($8,000) from the total amount of the mortgage payments I have made over the fifteen years ($22,036).

The tax bracket I used to estimate my tax savings was 45 percent. Note here, if you will, that I have paid $22,036 in mortgage payments and $10,500 in real estate taxes (both of which are deductible) but have saved only $10,141 in income taxes. Advantage, as we tennis buffs say, lender. On to the litmus test.

Total cash outlays	$61,636
Income tax savings	10,141
Net after-tax outlay	$51,495

How's that strike you? I'm net out of pocket half a century. Maybe I could recoup some of it if I sold the home. Let's see.

Projected sales price	$95,000
Less: Capital gains taxes (Assuming no repurchase) Federal tax (20% of my gain based on a tax cost of $25,200—the purchase price of $22,000 plus $3,200 worth of improvements—so the gain is $69,800)	13,960
Massachusetts (take my word for it) capital gain tax	3,001
Mortgage balance (Note no real estate broker's fee. This would be a further cut.)	8,000
Net cash from the sale	$70,039

Finally, we must see what kind of return I actually received. We do this by subtracting my net cash outlays from this net cash available from the sale.

Net cash from the sale	$70,039
Net cash outlays	51,495
Gain	$18,544

Dividing this last figure by the amount I have "invested" (the net cash outlays), I'd come up with a 36 percent return. For each of the fifteen years, my return would average 2.4 percent. Super. I would have been better off in a savings account.

But would I? I would have had to live somewhere. That would have cost me something. Here, at least, I get my money back. All of it. Plus a modest profit. And that is the true value of home-ownership as opposed to renting.

I took you through this lengthy discussion to prove a few points. First, homeownership provides, first and foremost, shelter, and only coincidentally an investment. (Contrary to my comments at the beginning of this chapter when I gave you the hype. But as you can see, there are indeed investment factors involved.) Second, its real advantage is the chance to recoup all the housing costs you have spent over the years. Third, the longer you own a home, the more mediocre will be your average rate of return because the larger the number of years you must divide that return over. Fourth, the psychic rewards may mean more than the monetary ones unless you trade your home every few years after getting a quick run-up in price (as some people do). Fifth, don't get deceived by the "sound" of things (as I led you into with my sweet-sounding thrust) but get the facts.

I invite you, if you are a homeowner, to go through the exercise I did with my own numbers to see really how superific your own home has performed for you. (That will deflate your ego.) Until you do, you may be under a mistaken impression that you've made a phenomenally great investment. I think you'll be surprised if you take the time to do it.

If you own a home and are looking to sell it, you can go through the calculations I did near the tail end of my epic tale to see what you'll net after taxes, mortgage repayments, brokerage cost and other costs (such as legal fees, moving, new furnishings, and so on). And, of course, you won't worry about the tax bite if you're going to repurchase another principal residence for the same or greater value as the home you're selling.

If you don't own a home and want to buy one, or if you own one and want to consider buying another, and you'd like to compare the costs of the two alternatives, you must do both a cash "flow" kind of analysis and an estimated Federal income tax comparison. These lessons were taught earlier, but if you need a refresher course, I'll give you a quick summation. Start with the cash outlays in each of the two situations by making two lists, one for each alternative. Include all of the cash costs that each alternative would entail. (Like rent or mortgage payments, real estate taxes, utilities, insurance, parking fees, maintenance items.) Compare the totals of the two lists, and you'll know which one is costlier cashwise. Then do an income tax estimate under both alternatives by using the format I gave you in the second part of this book, or do a quick and dirty: list all possible itemized deductions under each alternative; subtract your zero bracket amount; multiply your excess itemized deductions by your tax bracket rate in each of the two alternatives to guess at your tax savings; and finally, deduct those tax savings from your cash costs under each scenario to determine your net cash costs after income taxes.

By taking the time to go through these calculations for alternative housing, for the cost of getting from the home you are currently residing in to the one you may be contemplating, and for the profitability of your homeownership, you will have all you need to understand what housing does for you in financial terms. Don't be disillusioned. How else can you get free living with a cash bonus when you sell?

CHAPTER FORTY-ONE

DUST, TREES, BRICKS, PLASTER AND MACADAM

Investing in real estate that you do not use for personal reasons or that you may use strictly for business reasons takes on many faces. You can choose from buying land (usually referred to as "raw" land, which may mean it's either uncooked or rugged), interests in land (such as mineral rights, timbering or crops), a multi-family structure you partially occupy (a two- or three-family house), or rental property of other kinds (a condominium or cooperative apartment, an apartment building, an office block, a shopping center or a hotel or motel unit). Depending on which you choose, you are aiming at different objectives and may get different rewards. How selective you are and how you finance your deal also have major ramifications. The mix of all these factors will determine which layer of your investment program your real estate investment will fall into. It can fall into any of the three layers.

There are three types of rewards that can come to you from investing in real estate: (1) You may receive a net cash income. (2) You may receive a tax break. (3) You may receive appreciation in value. These ingredients of a return are not always separable, although some types of investments may give you more of one than of the other two, and some types of investments may give you some degree of all three. To name a few possibilities: investing in land may give you more appreciation return than income or tax break return; investing in oil or gas development rights (interests in producing wells) may give you more of both an income and a tax break but less of an appreciation return; investing in residential rental real estate may give you more in tax breaks and appreciation than in income. These are examples, and

I speak in generalities because so much depends on the specific location of the property, the numbers involved, and how you finance it. The point is that if your investment objective is income, you should look for the type of real estate investment that is most likely to provide income and structure the transaction in such a way as to maximize the income from the property. Sounds obvious, I know. But I hate to tell you the number of times I get asked point-blank, "Is this a good deal?" "Good for what?" I ask. In the abstract, there are no good deals or bad deals, only deals. Look at the potential the deal offers and your objectives, and mesh the two as best you can. At least for openers.

A few more comments in general before I give you a specific example. Investing in land may be speculative rather than conservative (which I bet is the image you have in mind). If the land is not in the heart of things or in the path of development or a new highway, you may wait a long time to get your price. Existing developments are more conservative than new ones. There may be interminable delays with new ones, or the town fathers may change the rules, or the development-money well may be dry, or no one may like to occupy the space you thought was fantastic. With an existing development, there is a history to go by. This may not be conclusive, but it helps. Look at the viability of the investment from an economic standpoint and don't get overcome by the potential tax breaks. They're nice to have as icing on the gingerbread, but they're not of utmost importance. Read the economic, demographic and social trends as best you can before you leap. Remember that real estate investments are less liquid than investments in securities, so you will need a long lead time before you actually get your cash out. Finally, having issued all of these cautionary brandishments, I must say that I am a big fan of real estate investing. It offers many advantages. They include the three kinds of rewards I've already mentioned, plus inflation protection and the use of borrowed money to "leverage" your investment. Leveraging can enable you to control more property with less money and to get a bigger percentage return on your invested dollars. This is the same concept I mentioned in Chapter 39 relative to options. It is attractive here because of the long-term nature of real estate investing and the fact that, in rental real estate, your tenant is putting money into your pocket every month by using his dollars to reduce the principal amount of the mortgage. This last feature has special value in two- and three-family houses in that your tenant may be paying a disproportionate part of the total mortgage and other costs, thus reducing your price for shelter. To my list of reasons for investing in real estate I want to add that this market has many players in it, just as does the securities market, and that having all those players helps you as an investor. There is some liquidity. There is activity. There is price visibility (you can find out what a property sold for). And there is a narrowed range of pricing that is set by the marketplace.

I would like to use a condominium unit as a specific example to show you how some of this works. By my own admission, having written a book on the subject, I am partial to condominiums anyway. I will give you a couple of reasons why shortly.

Assume that you want to invest in a $100,000 condominium unit that you will rent out. (Forget, for the moment, where you'll get the greenbacks.) You determine that the price is fair and that you can get $800 a month for rent. You also determine that real estate taxes run $2,400 a year and that the condominium's common charges (its maintenance fee) will cost another $2,400 a year. What else can you think of that will cost you money? Insurance for the inside of your unit and to protect you against liability claims. Let's say that will cost you $200 a year. Repairs or a new refrig? Let's say you allocate $500 for those purposes.

For a few paragraphs, I'm going to assume you're loaded and that you decide to pay all cash to acquire the unit. Your alternatives are to get help on the equity end to come up with the down payment (through some kind of pooling effort, which we will get to two chapters hence), or to turn to a lender or a combination of lenders to borrow from. More on this last alternative shortly. Back to my assumption: you will pay all cash and thus forego one of the tremendous advantages of real estate investing, the use of other people's money. Not that I recommend this all-cash approach; I just want to demonstrate a few things.

Here's what your acquisition of the unit would look like:

Purchase price	$100,000
Mortgage amount	0
Cash downpayment	$100,000

And here's what your annual cash flow (the cash income versus the cash outlays) would look like for the first year of your ownership:

Rental income	$9,600
Less:	
Real estate taxes	2,400
Common charges	2,400
Insurance	200
Repairs	500
Net cash income	$4,100

Terrific! You've just gone and invested $100,000, and you're going to get a 4.1 percent return on your hundred Gs. Who's crazy? Well, not me. Not yet, anyway. I said that one type of return you can get from real estate investing is an income return and that the three types of return may be blended in one investment in differing degrees. This is one of those mixed-bag types.

Turn your attention to the tax side of the first year's operations.

Rental income	$9,600
Less:	
Real estate taxes	2,400
Common charges	2,400
Insurance	200
Repairs	500
Depreciation	4,722
Tax-deductible loss	($622)

(In the heady world of cash-flow statements and of balance sheets, losses are commonly placed in parentheses to distinguish them from profits.)

What's going on here? The unit shows a positive cash net income of $4,100. But, for tax purposes, it shows a loss of $622.

Ah, the joys of tax reporting. Certainly, all of the operating expenses can be used for tax purposes as offsets against the rental income. On top of that, there is an allowance for this thing known as depreciation. Depreciation is a fictitious concept developed under the tax code permitting an annual write-off on your tax return for the allaged wasting away of the real estate you have just purchased. The code's theory is that at some time in the future the value of your unit will be reduced to zero for tax purposes. In reality, you and I know that if you bought right, the unit's value should be higher at the time you sell it than it is now. But the tax boys figure you can write some portion off each year to account for the wasting away of the asset. Under the tax code this allowance is known as Accelerated Cost Recovery System, shortened, as only the government can, to ACRS. Popularly, it is known as depreciation.

You are only allowed to depreciate an asset which is believed to be wasting away. Thus, land cannot be depreciated because (even the tax boys have caught on to this one) it will always be there. But a building is different. It should waste away. In your real estate investment, you must allocate the proportion of your purchase price that went to acquire the building and the portion that went to acquire the land. Normally, with a free-standing structure, you may end up with 20–25 percent of your purchase price being allocated to the cost of acquiring the land. In theory, when you buy a condominium unit you actually "own" no land, only a proportionate interest in it. This means, theoretically, you have a bigger portion of your acquisition price you may be able to depreciate. This is one of the reasons I'm partial to condominium investing. (The other is that there is some built-in management—an on-site superintendent or a professional manager—who can fix the leaky faucets and stuffed toilets that you, as an owner, would have to deal with.)

Let's assume we reasonably figure that 85 percent of your purchase went for the unit and 15 percent was allocated to the land. (I have seen allocations going much higher than this for the unit.) Eighty-five percent of $100,000 is the amount you can depreciate. You are permitted to depreciate this amount of $85,000 equally over eighteen years (which is how I got my $4,722 number in figuring tax loss—$85,000 divided by 18) or to use what is called an accelerated depreciation method which, in the first year, will allow you to deduct about twice what I used. The problem with using the accelerated method is that you get the higher depreciation in the first few years and lower depreciation in the last few years of the eighteen-year stretch. (True, that may be what you want.) Another problem is that if you use the accelerated method and sell the unit at a given time, you might get stuck with a bigger tax when you sell because all of the depreciation may be subject to ordinary tax rates rather than capital gains. (This is the stinger.) The choice you make requires input from an accountant or tax attorney. To be conservative and sure, I use the regular method.

What the depreciation does for you is to "shelter" up to $4,722 in income during the year. Each year for eighteen, if you hold the unit that long. No additional investment is required, it just rolls along merrily year after year. And there need not be any additional cash outlay on your part. You've bought the unit, and you get the depreciation along with it.

In my example the depreciation figure shelters the entire $4,100 of condominium net cash income from taxes. And, the remainder of the depreciation lets you shelter an additional $622 of income from any other source. You can shelter that amount whether it comes from earnings or investments. Or, if you can raise the rent or cut expenses by that amount, you can use it to cover the extra net income from the unit. In other words, this $4,722 of depreciation is there to be used fully to shelter income of that amount from tax—totally. That's a 4.7 percent tax-free return ($4,722 divided by the $100,000 invested, times 100). Now, then, how does that make your investment look? Suppose you're in the 30 percent tax bracket. You'd need a taxable return of 6.7 percent to give you an after-tax net equal to that tax-free 4.7 percent return (6.71 percent equals 4.7 divided by 70 percent—100 percent less the 30 percent that is your tax bracket). Of course, if you're in a higher tax bracket, you'd need a higher taxable return to equalize the 4.7 percent. If, for example, you're in the 50 percent tax bracket, the sheltered return of 4.7 percent would be equal to a taxable return of twice that, or 9.4 percent. You'd have to go out and find an investment which could produce that to leave you net after tax what your investment in this unit would leave you. Starting to look better?

Come with me down the road five years. To keep my demonstration simple, let's assume that everything increased at the rate of 5 percent a year for each of the five years and that there was no compounding. Your unit would then be worth $125,000. (Five percent of $100,000 equals $5,000, times five years of that increase.)

Your cash flow and tax situations would then look like this:

Cash		Tax	
Rental income	$12,000	Rental income	$12,000
Less: total expenses	6,875	Less: total expenses	6,875
		Depreciation	4,722
Net cash income	$5,125	Tax gain	$403

At this point in time, the net cash income has gone up by about $1,000, and the depreciation has continued to cover most of it. This shows that increased net rental income continues to be sheltered, as I suggested above. Taxwise, the unit is in almost a break-even posture.

You decide that you'd like to get some usable money from your unit, and you wonder how you might do this. You can either take out a mortgage on the unit, or you can sell it. We'll look at both to study the consequences.

Assuming that when you put a mortgage on the unit you'd like the net cash flow from the unit to cover the mortgage payments (thus you won't have to lay out any cash to get your hands on the money). How much of a mortgage will it support? We have net cash of $5,125 to apply to mortgage payments. The amount of the mortgage loan depends on the interest rates that are available and the number of years the lender will accept until full repayment. Assume that the maximum repayment period is twenty years instead of the twenty-five you had on your home mortgage in the last chapter. (Loans on investment property are normally written to come due in shorter periods than are loans on owner-occupied homes.) Let's also assume that the interest rate is 14 percent and that the lender will give you a direct-reduction mortgage. (Interest rates are higher on investment property than they are on owner-occupied property, and you may not get a direct-reduction loan.) According to the same trustworthy table I turned to in the last chapter to find monthly payments, the monthly payment for this loan will be $12.44 per $1,000 borrowed. How many thousands will the unit support? Multiply $12.44 times 12 to get the annual amount you will have to pay per $1,000 borrowed on these terms, and you get $149.28. Divide the net cash income of $5,125 by $149.28, and you get a little more than 34. This means that the net cash income will support a maximum mortgage of $34,000 at a rate of 14 percent over twenty years. That's how much you could borrow on those terms and have the unit's cash flow still support itself without forcing you to dig into your pocket. All we're doing is borrowing an amount which will wipe out the unit's cash flow. (This same reasoning applies if originally you had decided to borrow some portion of the purchase price instead of paying all cash. You had $4,100 to work with then. If you divided that number by the $149.28—assuming that mortgage terms were the same then—you'd get about 27. You could have borrowed as much as $27,000 on those terms when you bought the unit and still have it carry itself.) Back to my $34,000. Cashwise, you're break-even. Taxwise, you get an additional deduction for the interest on the loan, so you get an additional deduction of approximately $4,760, further adding to your tax loss.

There you sit. You've got the unit paying its own operating expenses. You've got a bigger tax write-off. And you've got $34,000 of tax-free money in your sweaty hands ready to invest somewhere else. And, on top of all that, you've got your tenant putting money into your pocket each month by covering the mortgage expense with his or her rent. What a lulu—not the tenant, the deal. (The same ideas apply to a two- or three-family house on the part you don't occupy.)

Suppose that instead of refinancing (read "borrowing"), you get fed up with all the money you're making and you decide to sell. The numbers would result in a net cash figure to you of $125,000. That's the sale price, and I'll assume no broker or other expenses just to keep it clean. You've made a profit of $25,000, or 25 percent, in five years. (That percentage figure could have been improved on if you had mortgaged the unit when you bought it.) The tax numbers will look like this:

Sale price	$125,000
Tax cost	76,390
Taxable gain	$48,610

The tax cost is the original purchase price of $100,000 less the five years of depreciation at $4,722 per year. The depreciation has enabled you to save taxes on your yearly income and to save taxes at your tax bracket (30 percent is what I gave you, but it may run to 50 percent). When sold, the profit will be taxed as a long-term capital gain having a maximum tax of 20 percent of the gain (ignoring the effect of the alternative minimum tax). You've saved paying tax on a current basis at a possibly higher rate and have converted the tax consequences to a capital gain situation with a maximum tax of 20 percent of the gain. (Again, ignoring the alternative minimum tax. Depending on the size of the gain, that tax might add a little to your bill.)

And, if you can believe it, you may be able to defer some or all of the capital gain tax. You can do a tax-free swap (exchanging your unit with someone else for another piece of real estate), or you might prefer doing an installment sale which will get you paid over time and have you taxed only on what you receive each year. These, like the rest of the tax matters, require professional help. But the possibilities are there.

And you thought real estate wasn't worth considering.

CHAPTER FORTY-TWO

SHELTER FROM THE REVENUERS

Everyone loves to beat the tax rap. Including me. There are two ways to do it: (1) by taking what I would consider to be sensible, cautious steps; (2) by declaring all-out warfare and investing in the most aggressive tax-shelter investments anyone can construct.

The conservative approach gives you plenty of opportunity to start with. There are basic tax-saving steps that every rational human being should automatically take. They consist of taking action with an eye on the tax consequences of what you're doing, and fitting in techniques that will accomplish your goals as well as save you taxes. Throughout, I have commented frequently on these matters. They include such things as using work-related benefit programs to their maximum, switching the sources of your investment returns to the more favored long-term capital gain variety, using your home as an investment and tax vehicle, applying trusts where you can, giving charitable gifts of appreciated property, considering the use of a custodial account or a trust for your children, shifting income from one year to the next or from one pocket to another, taking advantage of depreciation, and having an up-to-date estate plan. Each of these is a prudent step. Each will save taxes. And each is available to every one of us. You may be surprised, but these modest steps can save big tax dollars and do it without generating fear.

I cannot say that about those investments referred to as tax shelters or as tax-favored investments. Such investments are structured to use one or another part of the tax law's generous enticements. They may include investments in real estate, oil or gas, cattle, crops, equipment leasing, movies, and other esoteric stuff.

Earlier, I made my cynical comment about the tax law being Congress's reading of what social policy should be. That reading is nowhere more outspoken than in the tax-shelter provisions. These provisions are a determination of social policy and an attempt to use that determination to pull dollars into investments where they might not otherwise go. There are two sides to the coin. One is that because of risk or because the rewards may be too small, private investors have ignored putting money into areas where Congress feels they should. By definition, then, these investments are risky or unappealing. Congress steps in and, through tax breaks, gives incentives to those investors to pull in the money. These incentives may take a variety of forms. Everything from a total exclusion from taxable income (such as with the depletion allowance for oil and gas wells that are producing) to fast write-offs (such as speedier depreciation for some types of real estate investments) to capital gains treatment for what would be ordinary income (such as income produced from timber cutting). As you can see, the plums run all the way from total exclusion of income to deferral of income to a switch in the classification of income for tax purposes. I have no problem with accepting that these maneuvers might be necessary (although it may not sound that way). I'm trying to say that you should be aware of these manipulations. If you invest in a tax shelter at all, match your investment objectives with the objectives the deal is targeted at. Don't just jump when you see an ad for a tax-favored investment. Nearly everyone does. And don't pursue one of these beauties near the end of the year. That's the time when only the jackals are out on the street to scoop up money from all the procrastinators.

The vast majority of these tax shelters are financially unsound. They are not adequately financed. They are costly. (As much as 20–40 percent going to cover the costs of promotion and sales.) They are rife with conflicts of interest. Everyone's putting them together, whether those everyones have any past experience or success or not. And most of the deals are bult of gossamer. They are spun together by combining as many technicalities as can be squeezed into a sixty-page offering circular. In addition to the financial and operational risks and the risks that gave birth to the lures in the first place, there are other risks. One set has to do with the technicalities I was just mentioning. It's easy to get impaled when a technicality is finely honed. Another set of risks has to do with shifts in the tax laws. They can and do get changed. Still another set relates to the enforcement and auditing procedures of the IRS, which may be within the law but which also operate at the cutting edge of the law. And part of the financial risk is the possibility that, because of thin capitalization, there might occur an event that wipes out any tax breaks you expected and then some. These things, in the vast majority of instances, are treacherous at best.

There is one thing for certain—the promoter of the deal does very, very well.

For these kinds of deals, I like to say that if you need a tax shelter that badly, throw your money down a manhole and claim a casualty loss. You'll do just as well. For you should be looking at these things in terms of their economics and their financial viability and accept whatever tax breaks happen to come with the package.

This is not to say that all tax-favored investments must be on the brink of disaster or are run by sharpies. It is to set a tone so you'll know what you're in for. Why, there can indeed be some wonderful investments which take advantage of the tax breaks that the law permits. Just look at the real estate deal we discussed in the last chapter. There are tons of these opportunities. As that one shows, buying a condominium or another piece of real estate may be all you need to slice the tax toll.

But if you're really determined to wipe out your taxes, I've got a solution for you. Get religion. Become a church. If you become a church, you will not have to worry about income taxes, estate taxes or real estate taxes. Heaven on earth. But there is a catch. You can't take it with you.

CHAPTER FORTY-THREE

GROUP BEHAVIOR

You don't enjoy doing it alone. You're scared. You don't have the confidence. You lack the expertise, the time, the inclination, the money. You want to be a groupie. Fine. There's nothing wrong with that. I said way back in the first chapter of this part of the book that there are two ways for you to play this investment game, directly on your own or indirectly as part of a pool. Any of the reasons I've just cited can be a valid reason for your joining a pool. And every one of the investments I've covered in the past several chapters can be invested in by pooling your money with others.

What can you hope for in a pool? Any of a number of benefits. A large enough fund to provide diversification. Expertise. Professional management of your investment. Administrative services. Information.

What you can't expect is to be able to throw a dart and have that be your choice of a pool. Investigation and thought are necessary, just as they are with direct investing. And, once in, you can't turn your back on your investment and assume that all will end well. If you do, it won't. You've got to stay involved, pay attention, study, learn, and watch over your marbles. Inattention will get you exactly what you deserve—nothing.

Different pools do different things and have different advantages, drawbacks and mechanisms. Some of these are the result of the type of investments the pool makes. Others are endemic to the pooling process itself.

Let us start with pools that invest in real estate. Here you buy shares in a real estate investment trust. This type of group takes the money raised from the original purchasers of its shares or from purchasers of additional shares when they are sold by the trust, puts that money first into a huge pile, and then invests that pile in some kind of real estate deal. The trust's investments can change as it turns its portfolio over. The portfolio may consist of direct ownership of properties, a collection of a variety of mortgage loans, or some mix of the two, depending on what its charter authorizes. Since the shares of the trusts are publicly traded, you get some benefits. These include the ability to get into the game for a relatively few dollars, the ability to get out of the game because of the liquidity of the shares, and full disclosure of who you're dealing with and what's going on.

The drawbacks are those inherent in every type of pooled fund. They include your lack of control. You turn your money over to someone and he, she, or it runs it (but, you hope, doesn't run with it). There is the distance between you and the managers and between the managers and the investments. (Real estate is a localized market, but these guys are trying to do it on a national market. Even where the holdings of a pool are securities rather than real estate, it would do the managers good to make a point of visiting the companies—and most of them do.) Size can be important. (Too many dollars chasing too few good investments. Muscle freeze and inflexibility with too much money. Too much diversification because there are so many dollars to spread around.) There is also the requirement for management to outperform everyone else to keep your confidence and your money. This drive may result in ill-timed, ill-conceived, or irrational investment decisions to show performance. And some of these decisions may result in tax consequences to you that you weren't counting on. In short, to repeat, the kinds of problems you may have with an investment in any pool.

The alternative to buying real estate investment trust shares as a means of investing in a pooled real estate fund is to invest in a limited partnership. This is a method which is used primarily for tax-shelter investing because of the limitation on liability and the flow-through tax aspects, but it can be used to invest in anything. The advantages these partnerships offer are the ability to participate in a large pool with a small number of dollars (usually $1,000 or $5,000), to achieve some diversity, to have all the details handled for you, to be a totally passive investor, and to partake of what is supposed to be professional management. The drawbacks are those I gave you above on the real estate investment trusts plus a few more. Some of these deals are not publicly offered so the degree of disclosure may be pitiful. Some of the promoters in the trade should be out plying other lines of endeavors. The competition for deals is keen so the choices made may be questionable. The sales expenses may be high. And there is usually very limited liquidity to what you buy, so if you want or have to get out you'll go whistling. Where the partnership interest in publicly syndicated, the offering brokerage firm will offer to "make a market" in the partnership interests, but this does not commit them to buying it or finding a buyer. It is principally a moral issue that they will try.

The general partner is the head honcho and runs the show. You may have some concerns about him. Who is he? What's he done before? What's he take in fees?

I don't want to sound negative about the limited partnership approach. It can have merit, but has to be approached gingerly. My conclusion has been, many times, why not do it yourself? If you want a pool, why not find some of your friends and business acquaintances who have the same needs as you do and then structure your own deal? Whatever professional help you need can be bought. And the cost will be lower than the promotion fees and the skimming that accompanies those that are offered to you.

Turning to those pools that buy securities, I should name three different types of pools and what their characteristics are.

First, there are unit trusts. These are pools of interest-paying securities which self-destruct. Someone, a broker, puts a package of securities together at the outset and then sells a slice of the pie to a number of investors. The slices usually go for $1,000 apiece. The pooled securities were selected by a professional, and a professional does the bookkeeping and payment making. There is no active management of the pool after it is established. As the securities pay interest, the interest is distributed to the holders of slices in the pool. These payments may be made monthly, quarterly or semi-annually, as the investor chooses. As the securities mature or are called, the principal is paid to the investors. When all the securities have matured, poof goes the unit trust. Generally, these have their greatest use in holdings of long-term municipals. The unit trust is also used for corporate debt securities and only infrequently for U.S. government securities. Some brokers are now trying the idea on common stock holdings: a fixed but mixed bag of stocks is thrown in at the outset, and at a predetermined date the stock is sold and the proceeds distributed. So far, this application hasn't been joyously received by the investing public.

The traditional uses of the unit trust result in diversification and professional selection and administration. It is known in the trade that securities that can't be sold otherwise are put into such a trust and the public then snaps them up. Not all trusts have these castoffs in them. You must recognize that all you own is a share of the holdings of the trust. This is no different for any of these securities pools. In making your investment decision, you must realize this and look at the underlying portfolio securities. The sponsor of the unit trust may make a market in its units so you will have a limited degree of liquidity.

The position you hold in the last two pools I'll mention gives you total liquidity. One of these pools is a closed-end fund, and one is an open-end, or mutual, fund. Liquidity exists in the closed-end fund because shares of the fund are publicly traded. Liquidity exists in the mutual fund because the fund is bound to buy back your shares any time you want to redeem them. Shares in closed-end funds fluctuate in the marketplace. On any given day the share price may be more than or less than the net asset value which underlies the shares. No one can explain why most closed-end fund shares trade at a discount from this underlying value. A closed-end fund sells it shares initially, takes the money and buys whatever its charter authorizes it to invest in. There is active management of its holdings. No additional shares in the fund can be sold without the approval of its stockholders, and that is why it's called closed-end—because there is a limit on the number of shares in it.

An open-end or mutual fund continues to issue shares daily. Since all shares are sold at the established net asset value per share, no one is at an advantage or disadvantage. Some funds sell their shares directly to investors and charge no sales commission (no-load funds). Shares in other funds may be sold by brokers, who charge a commission as high as 8½ percent. It does not pay to buy the load funds simply for the privilege of having a broker sell them to you.

The advantages that closed- and open-end funds offer are the ones they tell you about in their literature. The diversification you get. The professional management you get. And the administrative services you get. The disadvantages are the ones I enumerated eons ago.

Both types of funds offer a wide disparity within their areas as to fund objectives, techniques employed to reach those objectives, types of investments, restrictions on investments, management background and depth, management and other fees and expenses, degree of diversification, portfolio size and concentration, management, philosophy, portfolio turnover, special services offered, and performance records. On the issue of performance, don't chase the smoking gun. Typically, the hotshot of the past year becomes the cold turkey of the current season. If performance is what you seek, check the records over a five- and a ten-year period. The late-August issue of *Forbes* magazine will give you an annual ranking of how they see performance.

What more can I say? There are funds for all seasons and for all tastes with all kinds of variables. I've already said some research will be necessary. Perhaps the best place to start is with the *Forbes* ratings. Then get reports and prospectuses on those you're interested in. The actual selection process may include all the consideration I named in the preceding paragraph.

Perhaps you'd like a do-it-yourself idea here, too. Try to organize an investment club and form your own pool. Information on such clubs can be had from any broker.

CHAPTER FORTY-FOUR

BAUBLES, BANGLES AND GREED

In this chapter you get the chance to reach out and touch something. These are my words regarding investments in tangible property. I should really say tangible personal property as distinguished from tangible real property. But no one calls real property tangible. Technically, the distinction is that personal property can be moved and carted around whereas real property stays put.

Do you like to have a Picasso hanging in your breakfast nook? Do you take pleasure in the feel of an oriental rug between your toes? The cool brilliance of a diamond rock hung over your throat? The jingle of gold coins rattling in your pocket? The sheen on that antique Dusenberg roadster idled in your garage? Stamps sticking to your fingers? Furs clinging to your breast? Chippendales clogging your sitting room? Stradivarius violins on your coffee table?

What kind of psycho case are you, anyway? Don't you know these gems are nuisances? That they may give you mucho pleasure but as investments they belong in the aggressive category? That the price of any one of them may obliterate the remainder of your investable funds? But if possess them you must, then investing in tangible property is for you.

Beyond the personal satisfaction, there may indeed be the potential for some financial rewards. These rewards must be identified along with the problems relating to ownership of these assets.

"They" tell you that to play in these markets you must have specific knowledge of the markets. I say you need knowledge to play in any investment market. "They" tell you to avoid fads, for, man, are there ever fads in these markets. I say you must avoid fads in any investment; march to your own tune. "They" tell you that you will incur some costs which add to the price of investing. I say there are costs related to every investment. True, there may be some extra costs incurred with tangible property. These may be for storage or to keep the item safe or to insure it. But some of these costs may also be applicable to real estate investments and maybe securities as well, depending on how you do your transactions. Granted, tangibles take up space or they wouldn't be tangible. That, for some, may be a nuisance. (I like to travel light. In my advancing years, I believe there are monstrous benefits in keeping the bulk of my assets liquid or in an intangible investment rather than in bulk.) "They" tell you that you will receive no income from these investments. And they're absolutely right. These investments can produce only one type of financial reward and that is appreciation in their price. As long as you know going in that that's your investment objective and only potential reward, fine. But you also must recognize that some of them (like gold, silver, diamonds) are merely commodities (albeit commodities with centuries of sex appeal) and that others of them may act like commodities. Any commodity is affected by the laws of supply and demand, and in this trade, those laws may be tinkered with. But I say: so they don't produce current income. So what? There may be investments of other types (such as some real estate and some stocks) which produce no current income. That's not terminal to the investment mode. It relates to your objectives.

Whatever "they" say, the main drawback here is liquidity. For some of the items I've mentioned there may be an active market and thus a visible price. This would include gold and silver where daily quotes are readily available. But for many of the other items, this cannot be said. There is no active market, there is no visible price. And for all these tangibles the market is not played in by very many players. So the depth of the market may be shallow. Then, too, the spread of commissions between the cost of the item you're buying or selling and the price you pay or get can be enormous. Enough of a spread to crush a Louis XIV chair. Any potential gains may be deluged by these commissions. Add to this the vast volatility in price that may come from sporadic sales, and you'll get some picture of the odds.

Tangible property may have a place in most investment programs, but a relatively very small place unless you're really a devotee of the cult, are the world's recognized expert on the subject, and can "control" your market.

To think that any of these investments (say, gold) can protect you from global disaster is nonsense. You can't eat it or drink it. You may be able to wear it (in spots), but it won't keep you warm and healthy. The defense of it may be impossible. If I had my choice, I'd rather have a Winchester so I could fend off the hordes of attackers trying to get my canned asparagus.

CHAPTER FORTY-FIVE

THE AMERICAN WAY

Everything we've been discussing will make you financially comfortable and make you rich slowly. It may make your net worth extra large. But it won't make you enormously wealthy if your definition of enormously wealthy really is to make an explosive mark on your balance sheet. To do that, and to get tremendous personal satisfaction, you have to pursue the American spirit and do your own thing.

I mean you can start your own avocation, second career, moonlight undertaking, or business. I can't convey the fun of it. I can't convey the satisfaction of it. I can't convey the challenge of it. I can't convey the freedom of spirit that it provides. I can't convey the thrills, the decision-making contests, or the learning curve. I can't convey the persistence required. But I can tell you that it is the most personally satisfying thing you could ever do, and that if it works, financially you'll be in command. Fortunes are still being made this way.

Not that you have to pursue these enterprises with the expectation of making your fortune. You can pursue them for the nonmonetary rewards as well as for the monetary ones. Not that you have to make an all-out assault and work from some grandiose master plan. Not that you can't set your sights somewhat lower and take a partial victory. All I'm doing is telling you of the joys, both psychic and monetary, that will be yours if you do it, even on a part-time basis.

Think of your knowledge, the things you know. Think of your skills. Think of the possible applications of your talents and of the needs that might be fulfilled by them. Think of a game plan. Come up with some reasonable beginning and go at it. Trial and error, patience and persistence will pay off as long as you don't risk all the family jewels on the first roll. This is where my career-counseling credentials end.

CHAPTER FORTY-SIX

GETTING STARTED

To succeed with your finances, you must proceed in a series of tiny steps. Each step should lead in the general direction of the next. But retain your flexibility with each new forward thrust.

You must have an overall framework to your affairs and some sense of direction in what you'd like to accomplish. I have tried to provide these for you and to encourage you to take over from here.

To advance from here, you must set some priorities. No one can do everything all at once. Follow my process of gathering, organizing, analyzing, defending and attacking in a review of your situation, and you will turn up the issues you must address. Interestingly, during this process, you will also realize without conscious effort that you already know what your priorities must be. Work on them one by one, and as you lick them, you will boost your confidence, seize control of your finances and live a financially rewarding life.

INDEX

Accelerated Cost Recovery System (ACRS), 221
Accelerated depreciation, 221–22
"Adjusted gross income," 85, 88
Alimony payments, 85, 86
Annuities, 62, 185
Apartment, as real estate investment, 217
Art, 234
Assets
  acquisition and tax cost of, 38–39
  capital, 83, 209
  definition of, 33
  examples of, 33–34
  liquid, 35–36, 37, 136
  listing, 33–34, 37–40
  market value of, 39
  non-liquid, 35, 37
  ownership of, 38, 128–30
  proportion of debts to, 48–49
  selling, 83, 95–96
  table of, 40
Automobile insurance, 107
  provided by employer, 60

Balance sheet, 65–66
  and employee benefits, 55
  function of, 53–54
Banks
  and certificates of deposit, 186, 189
  checking accounts, 186

money-market accounts, 167, 169, 178
  risk in investing in, 188
  savings accounts, 167
  and types of deposits, 186
Beneficiary, 126, 144
Benefit costs, 55
Bonds, 187–88
  "call" provision on, 191–92
  corporate, 188, 189–93
  coupon rate of, 191, 192
  dormitory, 188
  industrial investment, 187–88
  and maturity, 187, 192, 193
  municipal, 82, 95, 187–89
  revenue, 187
  risks in investment in, 188–89, 192
  U.S. Treasury, 186, 187, 188
Books on taxes or investments, 93
Borrowing money. See Loans
Budget, 65–68
  deficit, 77
  function of, 67
  income portion of, 69–71
  sections of, 66
  surplus, 77

Capital assets, 83, 209
Capital gains, 83, 178, 179
  long-term, 83, 95, 97